GETTING STARTED ON THE RIGHT PAW
BASIC DOG TRAINING

Introducing Your New Dog to Your Home, Other Pets and More!

EVERYTHING DOGS BOOK COLLECTION

By Mercy Lopez

Getting Started on the Right Paw Basic Training, Introducing Your New Dog to Your Home and Other Pets

Everything Dogs Series Book Collection

Mercy Lopez

This is a work of photography, videos, research and experiences that are based on true shelter dog stories. Any resemblance to actual persons/animals living or dead, events or locales is entirely coincidental.

All rights reserved. The morals of the author have been asserted. Copyright © 2019, by Mercy - Mercedes Lopez-Roberson

No photography or any part of this book may be reproduced in any form; by any electronic or mechanical means, including; information, storage files and retrieval systems without explicit permission in writing from the publisher.

Book design and published by:
photo-video journalist, author, educator, animal advocate, activist, SAG actress/stunt woman, model and ASCAP songwriter

Mercy Lopez
www.everythingdogs.net

ISBN ebook 978-0-9980415-3-7

About the Author

Mercy is a first generation Cuban/Spanish American, photojournalist, animal advocate, media influencer, foster mom, volunteer, dog rehabilitator, book author, educator and is vegan. What is really interesting about her animal adoption photography and videos productions, aside from the fact that she really captures the real person-

ality of the dogs, is that, she uses some of her original music in them.

Mercy's background in music, as a guitarist/singer/song writer, developed in her becoming an ASCAP (American Society of Composers) member and a recording artist with BMG in Berlin, Germany for 3 years.

"Show me" Video!

Binky & Sabien's "No Idea" Sunrise Music Video!

The Mercy Lopez Band Live Video!

Mercy is pictured here on the right, as a blonde, on set filming a Toyota Prius' commercial from the 90's, in South Beach!

She is originally from Miami, then South Beach, where she won a Harley Davidson in a beauty contest sponsored by Cristal Aguardiente and Venus Swimwear 1992. This led Mercy into modeling on the pages of Playboy, (as a blonde and a brunette), numerous videos, commercial work, BMG Germany Recording Artist, acting in soap operas in the Mexico DF with TV Azteca, as well as SAG acting jobs with: Oliver Stone's in *"On Any Givin Sunday"*; The Farrelly Brothers' in *"Something About Mary"*; Adam Sandler's in *"Water Boy"*; and Micheal Bays' in *"Bad Boy II" (as a* SAG/stunt action woman). Working in these industries gave Mercy a good understanding of working with lighting and composition for her own photography and video productions.

Mercy then sold her investment property, in Little Havana, Florida to relocated to West Palm Beach, Florida, where she practiced as a commodities broker and a Realtor. She jogged and walked her dogs twice everyday, found lots of dogs and develop a reputation as "The Dog Lady" in the neighborhood. By her coming across so many stray dogs, it led her to help dogs out many ways like: by volunteering and fostering at the local shelters and rescues. At one point (for a few years), she went every Sunday to her community shelter till closing. She even got locked in the kennel adoption floor a lot, because it was hard for her to leave. Helping dogs keeps her Mercedes/Mercy very busy and it is especially rewarding to her when, she see's the faces of rescued pets together with their new forever family.

With the great support she received from social media and happy adoptions, it encouraged Mercy to spend about 5 years of her time, into getting her new book collection just right to publish. It has more detail than, she has in her previously published 15 mini iBooks. It's everything she thinks that's important for every dog guardian or animal lover.

She admits that volunteering can be challenging work that, has left her with some very unsettling experiences. This is why writing these books brought Mercy lots of healing by honoring so many dogs she worked with and their memories here. It is apparent that, every dog she has worked with has deeply touched her heart.

Mercy says, "It's very important to attract attention by generating media interest in animal issues like: sterilization programs, dog training, assisting animals in our communities, finding successful homes and most importantly, to reduce animal intake and euthanasia in shelters everywhere". With photography, video and social media, she knows that we can reach the masses, for successful adoptions and sterilization. She sees positive improvements every year!

It is very apparent on Mercy's Facebook page, that her passion burns deep with enthusiasm and she is full of positive optimism.

She hopes that her work encourages you to help out animals in some way.

Just click on the blue links to check out some of her videos and get to know her awesome furry friends!

Avery's Adoption Video and Hannah's Adoption Video.

CBS "Pet of the Day" with Avery & Hannah

Facebook Live, CBS "Pet of the Day"

Mercy's Portfolio Pictures

On the previous page from left to right, going down:
- With Oliver Stone, on set filming "On Any Given Sunday"
- With Henry Winkler and Adam Sandler on set filming "Water Boy"
- Mercedes as Black Widow series model for Marble, Wizard and Max Comic Books, by Greg Horn
- With LL Cool Jay on "Any Given Sunday"
- With Lenny Kravitz
- Germany BMG "Show Me" music video.
- Mercy Lopez Band performing in Berlin
- Black Widow Cover
- Toyota Prius Commercial with a pink dog
- "Universal Soldier" with Jean-Claude Van Dam
- Guitarist for Luis Enrique, Universal music
- Playboy September 1992's "Girls of South Beach". With Mr. Olympia Bob Paris. Catalog work in Cancun, Mexico
- Pepsi

My Foster, Stella's Story

Stella's Story Video

Mercy's Singing Dogs Here!

Introduction

Everything Dogs Book Collection

Everything Dogs Series Introduction Video

Everything Dogs 15 Minutes Mini Movie Here!

Everything Dogs Collection Book Project is based on true shelter dog photography and video stories (with original music from the author-publisher), combined with detailed research of everything pet guardians and animal lovers should know about dogs.

Everything Dog's was designed to: enhance our relationship with dogs, reduce animal intake, assist in eliminate euthanasia numbers in shelters, educate on today's animal overpopulation situation in shelters in the United State's, encourage: fostering, volunteering, sterilization, adopting, basic dog training and humane holistic health maintenance animal care, even during a pet emergency.

All of the collections books contain many pet guardians tips that, can lead to an enhanced, positive, safe and loving relationship with your furry family member.

Proceeds of Everything Dogs Education Book Collection goes to animal rescue charity partners.
This book *"Getting Started on the Right Paw Basic Training - How to Introduce Your New Dog to Your Home & Other Dogs"* specifically goes over:

How to Pick the Right Pet Together as a Family, Statistics, What to Consider When Adopting a Dog, True Shelter Dog's Pictures and Video Stories Links, Children and Dogs, How to Introduce Your New Dog to Your Home and Other Exciting Pets, How to Doggie Proof Your Home and Yard, How To Get Ready for Your New Dog to Come Home, Safety, House Training, Chewing, Leaving Pets Home Alone, How to Avoid Bathroom Accidents, Basic Dog Training, Placement, Rewards for Your Dogs, Basic Commands, Leash Pulling, Heel and more!

Other Everything Dogs Book Collections includes:

Saving Shelter Dogs - True Shelter Dog Stories and Everything You Should Know" goes over in detail:

The Truth About Animal Shelters, True Shelter Dog Stories (with videos and full-color pictures stories), Statistics, Fostering, Volunteering, Anti-Tethering Law, Condition of Intake Dogs, Common Choking Collar Accidents, Lost, Stray and Found Animals, What We are Doing to Bring our Animal Intake and Euthanasia Numbers Down, Sterilization, Euthanasia, High-Risk Animals, Black Dog Syndrome, Kennel-Mates Save Lives, Foster Dog Stories, Playgroup-Playing for Life Program, Count Down to Zero Initiative Program, Pitbull History, Breed Specific Legislation (BSL), How we are Saving Lives in our Communities and more!

- **Dogs Holistic Health Main- tenance and Remedies Encyclopedia:**

This book goes over the details of: Dog Holistic Healing, Natural Alternatives, Essential Oils, Herbs, Natural Repellents, Different Skin Conditions, Hot Spots, Yeast, Staff Infection, Demodex, Natural Holistic Fleas and Ticks, Prevention and Natural Alternatives, Ears, Eyes, Teeth, Gums, Older Dog's Health, Super Healing Roots, Super-Greens Supplementation, Benefits of Basic Herbs, Herbal Tonic Remedies, Vaccines, Holistic Alternatives and Remedies, Heartworms, Natural Prevention for Flea, Tick, Heartworm and Mosquitos for your Lawn and Home, Homeopathic Do It Yourself Sprays, Vaccines, Medications, Foods You Can and Can Not Feed Your Dogs, Gluten-Free Grains, Prebiotic, Probiotics, Live Enzymes, Leaky Gut, Basic Nutrition Your Dog Needs on a Vegan Diet, Dog Health Maintenance and Holistic Natural Alternative Remedies, pH Balance, What is in Your Pet's Food, Nutrition, Vegan Food Full Color Pictures, and Recipes and much more!!!

- **Dog Emergencies** - What to do in a Common Pet Emergency:
Dog's Emergencies is a quick training manual to prepare you in case of a rescue emergency with your pet or any dog that may need your fast action assistance

It goes over: Most Common Pet Emergencies, How to Respond, Rescue Protocols, First Aid, What to do if your dog is Over-Heating, How to Perform Heimlich maneuver if your dog is choking, CPR/Cardiopulmonary Resuscitation on your pet, Safety demonstration videos more!

I hope that you will look at animal overpopulation in your own back yard, differently, and compassionately.

After volunteering at shelters, I am more aware about the truth that, takes place in animal shelters. I just wanted to share with you a little bit of what the dogs are like, based on my experience, their story and dedicate this to all the souls of animals that never walk out of a shelter alive. After collecting tremendous amounts of dog pictures, Everything Dogs books honor their memory in hopes that, it moves someone like you, to save a dog or help. No animals life should end shortly because, they don't have a home or space in the shelter.

Warning: This inspiring education book may cause a sudden urge to start saving dog's lives. You might even end up being a possible foster failure!

Open your heart to fostering, volunteering, donating and adopting. All animals can enhance your life, bring your happiness and even benefit your health!

Special Dedication to Binky

On June 1, 2011, I was walking my dogs before heading to a yoga class. My neighbor approached me with this beautiful black and white, female, Pitbull mix dog. He had just found her in the vacant lot next to us. He gave her to me because, he knew I was a dog person and saw me walking my two dogs every day, twice a day. I named her "Binky". She was about a year old, so cute, sweet and beautiful that, I could not resist, to immediately help her out. I brought her home, gave her food, water and took care of her, until I could hopefully get her back to her

owners. I got her immediately scanned for a microchip, but she did not have one, or any identification tag. I followed the legal protocol for lost and found dogs. I thought someone must be missing and/or looking for her because of the red collar she had on, so followed found dog protocol. I quickly starting to put up lost/found dog flyers and signs everywhere, so she would be visible for her family to find her. I took advantage of all the free ads in the major local newspapers. I also posted her picture on the Palm Beach County Animal Care and Control website page; under found dog like you are supposed to do, so that lost dogs can be reunited.

For days, we covered the entire area for miles to find her family, but no one had seen her before or knew who she belonged to, During this time, she became part of my pack of dogs and we fell in love with her.

After 10 days, I received a call from Animal Care and Control telling me to bring Binky in that, I can adopt her by putting a "reserve adoption hold" so I could take her back home with me.

When I brought her to Animal Care and Control, they asked me to wait for her while they checked her out privately. When they came back out, I was handed Binky's new collar and leash. I was told that Binky had to be put on a 10-day hold at the shelter to allow her legal guardian the opportunity to find her and start the 10 day process again. I was heartbroken. I was even more confused when, they told me that, I could not see or visit her while she was there. I thought How is her family going to find her? This was a very difficult realization. While I was there I observed how our community "kill shelters" are understaffed and under-budgeted. This, in turn, lacks to provide animals the attention, space, care they need and deserve.

City commissioners set out budgets for county departments and the last departments they consider funding are the ones that don't have a voice; like the animal service divisions known as animal control shelters in our community.

Finally, Binky's 10 days of being locked up in an unfamiliar scary kennel were over. I returned to Palm Beach County Animal Care and Control to rush my adoption application through; to get my "Stinky Binky" out. They told me again that, I could not see her and I would have to wait for an inspector to come out to my property (this took another 2 weeks). Finally, the inspection was complete. At this point, she was ready for surgery to get spayed/sterilized for final adoption with me. After her surgery, I still could not see or take her home. Apparently, she was bleeding internally, due to a towel she ate that, she

was still passing. I believe she eat the towel out of boredom, mind deteriorating and by not getting the attention she mentally and physically needed in a confined kennel space for such a long time. During this time, she developed Canine Infectious Respiratory Disease (CIRD), also known as Kennel Cough or a doggie cold. It's very similar to a human cold and very common. If she had the Bordatella vaccination given by her previous owner veterinarian, it would have prevented her from getting sick. Her time was running out at the shelter, when, I finally got a call saying that, "if you want her, then come get her now!".

Of course, I rushed to pick her up! On June 21, 2011, she officially became a member of our family. This was the longest month of my life. Aside from what she went through, her dramatic experience of being separated from me like that, but also she was

taking up unnecessary space in a kill shelter that, could have kept some dogs alive.

Everything Dogs Series Introduction Video

Check out a video clip of when Binky was given back to me and the special magical connection we had. How she recognized me and how we felt about one another. She was so excited and happy.

Through volunteering at a shelter, I later became friends with that same staff member who gave Binky back to me. She said she remembered that moment because, she had never seen a dog be so happy being pick up like that before; showing so much love to a stranger. Not knowing that, I had her with me for a short while and brought her in.
Soon after this experience, I decided to look into how I could help animals in my community at this particular kill shelter, even though I had volunteered

at other local animal rescue organizations. The more I saw, the more I realized that I had to somehow do more! Binky opened my eyes to how animals suffer in shelters because, of the current system in place and lack of sterilization. People say it is difficult to help out, so they just don't help out at all. We can change this attitude by showing in these books that, there are many different ways to help animals in dire need in your area. By giving a little bit of your time, love and affection to a shelter, or rescue organizations we can turn this awful animal overpopulation situation into a more positive one.

Binky was four years old when in the middle of the night she mysteriously started coughing up blood. The morning before she went for a jog alongside me as, I rollerbladed up the street, of course, I immediately rushed to get her the best help that, I could. I was scheduled to filming CBS - Channel 12's "Pet of the Day" that next morning. I was faced with having to drop my Binky off at the veterinarian to run

some tests and be separated from her for the first time since, our animal control experience. She had veterinarian check-up's a month before, showing that she was healthy. They gave a Heartworm preventative treatment injection for her first time. With this being said, I could not imagine anything being wrong with her but wondered if the heartworm prevention shot had something to do with this.

I took Binky to 4 different veterinarian specialist and we gave her every test that could help her available. No test or doctor could explain to us why her lungs were filling up so fast! They took out a minimum of 850 cc's of bloody fluid from her lungs each time (above pictures). She needed five emergency surgeries to drain the blood out of her lungs.

She also had two blood transfusions from "Apollo" GTS Husky Rescue; shown on the following page.

Apollo and I on "CBS Pet of the Day" Video!

During the course of the next ten days of her suffering, Binky could no longer lay down. It was as if she was drowning and suffocating from the blood filling up in her lungs. We could not sleep at all from holding her up so that, she could get some relief and rest while sleeping sitting up. Her lungs continued to refill faster every day with more blood, every breath for her was a struggle. You could hear the liquid build-up gurgling in her lungs. It was devastating for our family. Dr. Martin from Jupiter Animal Health Clinic worked with her endlessly, hoping that we could find out what was wrong with her to save her.

Some of the tests available would take two weeks for the results to get back to us. Time Binky didn't have. We treated her with vitamin K, thinking maybe she ate some poison and with "Yunnan Baiyao" (a hard to find Chinese herb, used during the Vietnam war to help stop bleeding). It changed the color of the fluid in her lungs, as you can see in the pictures shown above.

We did our best to figure out the mystery of why her lungs were disintegrating like gel. It was killing her! During this time, I learned that the veterinary field had its limitation. This may have been beneficial for my Binky at the time.

On November 21, 2014, Binky went into her last emergency surgery. Her last specialist veterinarian had installed tubes with knobs on each side of her, into her lungs in desperate measures to save her. This was so that, I could drain out the excess fluids in her lungs and help her breath. Her lungs kept on filling up with more bloody fluid, faster each day. We knew it was a very dangerous and sensitive procedure, but we thought this could help buy more time while we find out what was wrong and how to treat her. She needed medical intervention. We were running out of options for fighting off blood infections and transfusion risks. Her doctor said that she tried to take 2 breaths and died coming out of the anesthesia from surgery. I had a few moments with her and saw all the knobs and tubes sticking out of her in the attempt to save her. I never saw a dog fight so hard to live! I have never done so much in an attempt to keep a dog alive in such a short period of time.

After the necropsy, which is an autopsy for dogs, the doctor's opinion of the cause of death was idiopathic, meaning "unexplainable". They found that the blood clots and infection from the blood in her lungs was conclusive with what were going on with her. I still have no explanation as to what happened to my Binky. We could not find out why her lungs reacted this way. Maybe if there was more research, Binky would have lived a long life. I wish that we could have at least know what happened that, caused her lungs to disintegrate into a gel.

The mystery of what happened to my Binky still haunts me and remains in my memory. This experience still haunts me!
Because of what I have learned about the overall mentality of our government that mandates exces-

sive vaccines, the animal maintenance care industry (controlled by animal pharmaceuticals, plus large pet foods corporations preservatives in packaged foods) is possibly poisoning our pets. I believe that there are links to why so many dogs are commonly getting cancer at alarming numbers.

I know that there is a great deal of room for research and improvements for the advancement of veterinary medicine. I had another dog; "Ralph", that also had issues with lung cancer; as well as my "Joy Bird", that died of cancer. One of my dogs, "Hawkeye", died from eating a commercially sold rawhide. Manufactures knows rawhide commonly kills dogs and they continue to sell them! I'm thinking, "Could some of this be relevant to the pet foods that we feed our pets? Maybe there is a link with vaccines? Do you wonder too?

I now look at everything pertaining to dogs' health differently since, my experience with Binky. I question the dog health industries, the consumer products that are made available and advertised in today's modern convenient package food industry. So, I did extensive research for my own dogs' health and maintenance so that I can bring to you **the Dogs Holistic Health Maintenance and Remedies Encyclopedia"** book. I highly recommend for: health wellness conscious animal lover friends, .

Binky's passing away inspired me in many ways. Aside from helping at dog shelters and I also took a "foster challenge". I fostered five dogs in honor of the five surgical attempts to try to save Binky. As of now, I have surpassed that goal and have found many pets awesome safe homes. I now hope to raise money and to promote animal awareness with Everything Dogs Book Collection Project to help families and pooches!

My last picture with my "Binky" (bottom right) after her 4th surgery attempt trying to save her.

Binky Rounding Up Chickens!

Sabien & Binky Singing Together!

Ralph & Rodger
Love you & always in my heart, RIP.

I've had other dogs than Binky that had suffered from lung cancer and wonder why it is so common for dogs if they don't smoke. Could it be linked to the food that is sold to us commercially that is loaded with toxic preservatives, the additives, synthetic ingredient for the manufacture to meet the standard of nutrition to be sold to us because they are cooked in such high temperature that it kills the natural nutrition and causes harm?

Special Thanks

I want to thank my: Binky, Sabien, Hawkeye, Joy Bird, Mac, Ralph, Blankie, Benji, Broggie, Harley and Davidson. As well as my foster failures: Juno, Pretzel, Rodger, Mindy, and Coco for continuing to inspire me. They filled my heart with love.

I wish everyone could experience as many awesome memories with their furry family members too!

Thank you for taking the time to invest in your dogs and for your interest in the world of Everything Dogs!

Kim Tunney Johnson

I want to give recognition to this very talented, speedy, co- proofing editor. She is very sharp in the field of being a paralegal and is always multi-tasking. She has full custody of her adopted, sweet, beautiful granddaughter "Karina". She used to have more time to foster urgent status dogs and help out at the shelter. She helped save "Hope", a blind dog's life, that is now happily re-homed. Kim was a victim of her own dog being stolen by a burglar from home. She has never fully recovered from the loss of her furry loved one. She is an animal activist and is always helping out dogs; in the best ways that she can.

Disclaimer

Everything Dogs Book Collection is based on true rescue dog stories. It is intended for public education, to help families develop a lasting and healthy relationship with their pets. I feel if people can implement some of the information in these books, we can compassionately bring our animal intake and euthanasia numbers down in high kill shelters.

The publisher and author are not responsible for any specific health, or any allergy needs that may require medical supervision and not liable for any damages, or negative consequences from any treatments, actions, applications or preparations to any pet or person in regards to the reading or following any of the information contained in this book.

For diagnosis or treatment of any medical situation, always consult your own professional veterinarian immediately.

Neither the publisher nor the individual author shall be liable for any physical, psychological, emotional, financial or commercial damages. Including, but not limited to: special, incidental, consequential or other damages. You are responsible for your own choices, actions, decisions and results.

References are provided for informational purposes only and does not constitute an endorsement of any websites or other sources.

Readers should be aware that the web links listed in this book may change. No warranties or guarantees are expressed or implied by the publisher's choice to include any of the content in this book.

Table of Content

Getting Started on the Right Paw Basic Training, Introducing Your New Dog to Your Home and Other Pets ---1

Everything Dogs Series Book Collection ----------------1

Mercy Lopez --1

About the Author 3

"Show me" Video! --4

Binky & Sabien's "No Idea" Sunrise Music Video! ---4

The Mercy Lopez Band Live Video! ----------------------4

Avery's Adoption Video and Hannah's Adoption Video. ---8

CBS "Pet of the Day" with Avery & Hannah -----------8

Facebook Live, CBS "Pet of the Day" ------------------8

Mercy's Portfolio Pictures ------------------------------------9

Stella's Story Video ---11

Mercy's Singing Dogs Here! -----------------------------11

Introduction..12

Everything Dogs Series Introduction Video ---------12

Everything Dogs 15 Minutes Mini Movie Here! -----12

Special Dedication to Binky -----------------------------19

Everything Dogs Series Introduction Video ---------- 24
Apollo and I on "CBS Pet of the Day" Video! -------- 27
Binky Rounding Up Chickens! ------------------------------- 31
Sabien & Binky Singing Together! ---------------------- 31
Ralph & Rodger -- 33
Special Thanks -- 34
Kim Tunney Johnson -- 35
Disclaimer -- 36

Table of Content 38
Chapter 1 47
Getting Started on the Right Paw 47

Puppy Mill Statistics -- 49
Puppy Mills --- 50
Where are Puppy Mill Puppies ------------------------- 53
Common Puppy Diseases ------------------------------- 58
and Impairment -- 58
Happy Puppy Mill Dogs ----------------------------------- 59
Onyx's Puppy Mill Bust Story Video! ------------------ 59
J-Lynn --- 60
Chloe --- 61
Papa Luigi -- 62
Patellar Luxation in Dogs -------------------------------- 63

Chapter 2 65
Picking the Right Pet Together as a Family and What to Consider 65

My Story of Not Being Able to Keep My Husky Broggie! -- 70

What to Consider When Getting a New Pet --------- 72

Puppy Snowie's Adoption Video! ----------------------- 72

Make Sure you can Have Pet's Where you Live --- 75

Your Dogs Exercise and Bathroom Needs ----------- 76

Apartment Living Arrangements ------------------------ 79

Tips on Securing Your Property for Your New Pet!- 81

Make Sure You Can Afford and Keep a Safe and Clean Home Environment for Your Dog --------------- 84

Maintenance Expense ----------------------------------- 87

Traveling Tips! -- 91

First Aid Kit --- 93

Chapter 3 96
Different Dog Breeds Shelter Stories ... 96

Blue's Adoption Video ----------------------------------- 97

Coda -- 99

Lucky --- 99

Dizzy -- 99

Ice Cream's Adoption Video! ------------------------------------100

Icee --100

Vonda's Adoption Video! ---------------------------------102

Ghoast's Adoption Video! --------------------------------103

Beisha ---105

Sandy's Adoption Video! ---------------------------------106

Rodger Dodger's Special Adoption Video! ---------109

Coco Bean Adoption Video! ----------------------------110

Stella's Story Video! --110

Chapter 4 111
Tips for Children with Dogs 111
Chapter 5 122
How to Introduce Your New Dog to Your Home and Other Pets 122

How to Get Ready for Your "New Dog" to Come Into Your Home--124

How to Doggie Proof Your Home Inside and Outside! 128

Pools Safety--130

First Car Ride Safety---132

What to do When You Get Home with Your New Pet- 137

Chapter 6 145
Introducing Your New Dog to Your Existing Pets! 145

Resource Guarding---------------------------------------152

Common Signs of---153

Resource Guarding---------------------------------------153

Resource Guarding Tips ---------------------------------154

Tips for Introducing Your New Dog ----------------------155

to Your Cat!--155

Introducing Your New Dog to Your Chicken--------159

Two Person Introduction --------------------------------162

Chewing House Training---------------------------------163

Puppies Destroying a Pillow Video! -------------------164

Chapter 7 168
Leaving Dogs Home Alone 168

Crate Training--169

Putting Belonging Away ---------------------------------171

Going for Walks ---174

Dog Collar Caution --------------------------------------175

Toy Precautions ---176

Toys and Treats You Shouldn't Leave Your Alone Pet With---179

How to Avoid Bathroom Accidents--------------------180

Home Alone Pet Ideas------------------------------------182

Chapter 8 183
Basic Dog Training 183

Placement --184

Training with Treats--------------------------------------186

Portion Control---189

Regimen--189

Training Sessions--190

Collar Choices ---194

Check Chain and Martingale--------------------------194

Check Chain ---195

Harness --196

Police Leash ---197

Choke Collar Training-----------------------------------197

Basic Commands ---------------------------------------198

Name---198

Name, Let's Go--198

Name Heal---198

No Sir or Ma'am---199

Sit and Stay --199

Wait, Stay and Okay -----------------------------------199

Down ---199

No Jumping---200

Eye Contact --203

Sit, Eye Contact and Stay -------------------------------------204

The "Sit" Command ---206

The "Down" Command --209

Lay Down Under the Bridge------------------------------------212

"Lay Down" Hand Commands ---------------------------------213

"Play Dead!" or "BANG!" --213

Leash Pulling---216

The "Heel" Command---219

9/4/13 Urgent status; this 3 years old, Mastiff female only had 48 hours to find a foster or adopter when I took this picture at the shelter.------------------------222

Feeding Your Pets --223

Puppy Feeding Training Video!-------------------------------223

"Give Me Five", "Paw" or "Paws Up" -----------------------224

Scheina--225

The "Come" Command ---226

The "Roll Over" Trick --229

The "Stay" and "Up" Command ---------------------------230

Mix It Up a Bit and Have Fun --------------------------------231

Canine Good Citizen -- 232
Schutzhund -- 236
Schutzhund Training Video! ------------------------------------- 236

Chapter 9 238
Dog Attack Facts 238

5 Dog Breeds That Bite but Are Almost Never Reported -- 242

Walking Safely -- 243

Prevention, Defense and Protection ------------------- 244

What to do When You See a Loose Dog ------------ 250

Most Common Signs Dogs Give Before Biting ---- 252

in Any Situation -- 252

What to do if a Dog is Heading Towards You Aggressively --- 256

Protection --- 258

What To Do Before a Dog Starts to Attack You! --- 258

How to Defend Yourself From an Attacking Dog -- 261

How to Stop a Dog From Continuing to Attack a Victim -- 264

How to Stop a Dog Fight --------------------------------------- 267

with 2 People -- 267

Stopping a Dog Fight --- 268

With 1 Person ---268
What To Do Someone Gets Bitten by a Dog -------270
How to Avoid a Dog From Being a Dangerous Liability ---271
Spay and Neuter --273
About Your Dog--276
Exercise Your Dogs --276
Train Your Dogs ---277
Constrain Your Dogs ---------------------------------------281
Limit Exposure to Untested Situations or Places -284
Dog Parks--286
Good-Bye --287

Chapter 1
Getting Started on the Right Paw

Remember that different breeds, have different

needs. All dogs have their unique personalities. You should consider picking a pet that fits your lifestyle now and what you're into the future. Let this chapter guide you in making the transition into pet guardianship successful and positive for your family and other pets that you may currently have.

Let's start by getting you familiar with what Puppy Mills are, and the possible risk you could expect with your new pet if he/she came from a mill.

Puppy Mill Statistics

- An estimated **167,388 breeding dogs** are currently living in the United States Department of Agriculture (USDA) licensed commercial facilities for breeding purposes at this very moment.

- There are an estimated **10,000 puppy mills** in the United States (this includes both licensed and unlicensed facilities).

- Over **2 million puppies are bred** in mills each year.

- An estimated **5 million dogs** are euthanized in shelters every year. Hopefully, this number will continue to decrease.

- Thousands of commercially bred puppies are shipped and sold to pet stores each year.

- These statistics are sourced from the Humane Society of the United States (HSUS) 2014 Puppy Mill Facts Figures report (available here) and the American Society for the Prevention of Cruelty to Animals (ASPCA) Pet Statistics (link here).

Puppy Mills

- Puppy mills are dog breeding operations that put profits over the health and the well-being of dogs.

- Puppy mills may be large or small. They may be licensed by the United States Department of Agriculture or unlicensed. To sell to a pet store, the breeder must be licensed. Many still sell to pet stores without a proper license.

- Puppy mills can house hundreds or thousands of dogs. Smaller does not necessarily mean better. The conditions in small facilities can be just as cruel as larger ones.

- Puppy mills are everywhere. There is a large concentration in the Midwest. Missouri has the largest number of puppy mills in the United States. Amish and Mennonite communities (particularly in Ohio, Indiana, and Pennsylvania) that also have large concentrations of puppy mills.

- Puppy mills breed all types of dogs everything from; Labrador Retrievers, Boxers, English Bulldogs to teacup Yorkies. You can find nearly every breed.
- Breeding parents spend their lives in 24-hour confinement in cages. It is common to see wire cages stacked on top of each other. They generally do not

have protection from heat, cold, or inclement weather.

- Dogs in puppy mills live in dirty unsanitary conditions.

- Dogs living in puppy mills receive little to no veterinary care. Puppy mill owners often provide veterinary care without anesthesia or veterinary training.

- Mothers are bred every heat cycle and are usually killed when they can no longer produce.

- Many puppy mills do not practice humane euthanasia. Dogs are killed in cruel ways; including shooting or drowning.

- Puppies are taken from their mothers too young and can develop serious health or behavioral issues; due to the conditions in which they are bred and shipped. This leads to expensive veterinary bills, heartbreak and stress for their owners.

- The bottom line is that puppy mills are all about profits. Any money spent on veterinary care, quality food, shelter or staff to care for the dogs' cuts into the breeder's profit margin.

Where are Puppy Mill Puppies

- There are two primary sales outlets for puppies bred in puppy mills: pet stores and the internet.

- Nearly all puppies sold at pet stores come from puppy mills. Pet stores are the primary sales outlet for puppy mills and are essential for keeping puppy mills in business.

- Both licensed and unlicensed mills sell to pet stores (many mills sell to pet stores without the required license and are not held accountable).

- Puppies are bred in mills and then shipped all over the country. For example, puppies bred in the midwest may be shipped on trucks to southern California or Florida.

- The shipping conditions are inhumane. They can be forced to go up to 12 hours without food or water. They are confined in a small space where diseases can be easily transmitted. Many puppies do not survive.

*** The information on this page and puppy mill FAQs has been compiled based on first-hand experience with the rescue and rehabilitation of* dogs from puppy mills, years of researching USDA inspection reports and regulations, investigation of pet stores and the source of their dogs, and resources provided by national organizations with significant expertise on the puppy mill industry, including the HSUS, the ASPCA, and Best Friends Animal Society.

A puppy mill is a large-scale commercial dog breeding facility where profit is given priority over the well-being of the dogs. Puppy mills usually house dogs in overcrowded and unsanitary conditions without adequate veterinary care, food, water or socialization. To maximize profits, female dogs are bred at every opportunity with little-to-no recovery time between litters. Puppy mill puppies often, as young as eight weeks of age, are sold to pet shops or directly to the public via the internet. They are also sold through newspaper ads, as well as at swap meets and flea markets.

Again, puppy mill dogs are often kept in cages with wire flooring that injures their paws and leg. It is not unusual for cages to be stacked in columns. When female breeding dogs reach a point of physical depletion that, they can no longer reproduce, they are often killed.

Puppy mills focus on profit and the dogs are often bred with little regard for genetic quality. Puppy mill puppies are prone to congenital and hereditary conditions including; heart disease, blood, and respiratory disorders. Also, puppy mills puppies often arrive in pet stores and at their new homes with diseases, or infirmities ranging from parasites to pneumonia.

Puppies are removed from their litter-mates and the mothers at a young age. They can also suffer from fear, extreme shyness, aggression, anxiety, and other behavioral problems.

Because so many of these breeders are operating without oversight, it is impossible to accurately track them or to know how many there truly are. The legal definition of a "puppy mill" is accurate. Be careful because you could be fooled by pet store owners who show you legitimate papers or licenses to prove that their dogs are from humane sources. The fact is that most responsible breeders would never sell a puppy through a pet store because they want to screen potential buyers to ensure their puppies are going to a good home.

Illness and disease are common in dogs from puppy mills. A large portion of puppy mill operators often fails to apply proper practices of removing sick dogs from the general population, therefore spreading illness and disease.

Common Puppy Diseases and Impairment

Congenital and hereditary conditions like: giardia, parvovirus, distemper, upper respiratory infections, kennel cough, pneumonia, mange, fleas, intestinal parasites, heartworm, chronic diarrhea, epilepsy, heart disease, kidney disease, musculoskeletal disorders (hip dysplasia, luxating patellas, etc.), endocrine disorders (diabetes, hyperthyroidism), blood disorders (anemia, Von Willebrand disease).

Happy Puppy Mill Dogs

Onyx was one of the 366 counts of animal abuse puppy mill cases in Georgia, Cherokee County. Here is the video of his story and my time with him. GTS Husky Rescue, Jupiter, Florida.

Onyx's Puppy Mill Bust Story Video!

J-Lynn

A Manchester terrier, 7 lbs., about 1 year-old here. She was found as a stray and turned into Palm Beach County Animal Control. She then went into foster with a rescue. She became ill when the veterinarian discovered she had 2 dead puppies still inside her. She is better now and happily adopted by Blessed Paws Rescue, Lake Worth, Florida!

Chloe

From Miami Dade County Animal Services. A friend of mine (YM) from Miami, Florida assisted by going down to the shelter to evaluate Chloe and put an adoption hold for another friend in Mount Dora, Florida (MP), that adopted her. She fell in love with her pictures. She is a Manchester terrier, 7 lbs., about 1 year old at the time. She gets to travel and lives with 2 other dogs!

Papa Luigi

Papa Luigi was an urgent status and on the PTS (put to sleep) list because, he had behavior issues. As time was running out, I stepped up to foster him. During this time, I learned he had severe separation anxiety and barked excessively. We successfully found him a great home. His new family took him to a veterinarian and found out that, Little Papa Luigi could not see because, of a disorder, he had with his vision. He also has Patella Dystocis and ended up having heart surgery too. With all these thing wrong with him and not having someone to understand all his special needs, till his forever family came into his life. He is now on the road to recovering thanks to his new family.

Patellar Luxation in Dogs

This occurs when the dog's kneecap (patella) is dislocated from its normal anatomic position in the groove of the thigh bone (femur). When the kneecap is dislocated from the groove of the thigh bone, it can only be returned to its normal position once the quadriceps muscles in the hind legs of the animal relax and lengthen. It is for this reason why most dogs with the condition will hold up their hind legs for a few minutes.

Chapter 2
Picking the Right Pet Together as a Family and What to Consider

Take your time while making your decision of getting a new "forever" pet. Make time to look around at different local shelters and rescues. You can get a list of adoptable dogs from their website online, and you can call them up to ask about getting more information. However, it's always best for you to just go there with your family members, or people that, you live with. Even bring your existing dog for a meet, and greet with their new potential forever brother or sister to see if they would get along!

Make certain the breed's personality and any special needs of the dog you are choosing is right for you, your lifestyle and the people you live with for the years to come. Different dogs have different needs and they are all unique and special. If you choose to adopt a pedigree dog, make sure you get them from a recognized American Kennel Club (AKC) registered breeder with certification, including up to 5 generations of family lineage history, documented vaccinations, and all medical information.
It is highly advisable to have your veterinarian to do a physical on your new pet. Many people pose as legitimate breeders, but are not. They will scam you into giving them as much money as possible for the

dog. They will make you feel like you are getting a great deal. These people don't have any business to rightfully do this incriminating act of reproducing living dogs. So buyer beware!

Most rescues require potential adopters to complete an online adoption application, and will have it verified before an interview, or potential meeting and greet with the pet. This helps to determine whether they are a qualified adopter and if the dog personality and family make a good fit together. They may need some time before it is approved. A home inspection can be a standard requirement.

Rescues want to know: if where you live allows dogs or has any breed restrictions, what kind of experience you have with dogs, what will the dog's life be like with you and if you make a good save fit with the dog., Your veterinarian will be contacted regarding medical histories of past, present pets, heartworm maintenance. Regular shelters do an adoption application with a quick background check and maybe a home inspection if adopters have had pervious complains.

Feel free to call your local adoption facility to find out what their adoption procedure is. This way you are prepared ahead of time.

If you adopt your new pet from a source, other than a shelter or rescues, make sure it is legal. Again, you are recommended to take your new pet to a veterinarian for a **wellness check,** as soon as possible. This way you can have a better idea of what to expect from your new fur child. If the dog is from a shelter, rescue, certified breeder or trainer, I still recommend to have a professional veterinarian look at your new pet, so you don't later regret it. This is only my opinion: based on my experience! This would also alleviate any worry about your pet condition, or unnecessary expenses before you are responsible for all your new dog's medical expenses.

If you live with someone else, bring everyone from your household to meet your new potential pet. Sometime this may take a couple of visits. This should be a family decision done together. Everyone should be involved in picking your new pet.

My Story of Not Being Able to Keep My Husky Broggie!

The picture above is me at 17 years old with my Husky, Broggie. I worked and saved money to get myself my dream dog for $200. I found her in a newspaper ad. I could not resist. The breeder did not take any of my information, or verify if I could even have a dog where I lived or visit my home. He allowed to picking any puppy I wanted from the litter. Broggie was about 2 months old when I brought her home. Even though I contributed to house rent to my mother, did not allow me to ever keep my Broggie in the house. So she would get lots of ticks in her ears, and I had to spend lots of time to take care of this issue. We did not have the internet back in 1987 to collect valuable information on dog education, like we do today. Broggie & I use to spend the entire weekends and do everything together. I would take her to Crandon Park Beach in Miami for walks, grab a bagel for breakfast, did pizza runs and Velvet Cream donuts in Coconut Grove. We went everywhere together. She was my best friend. We were so happy together and inseparable!

One day my mother found Broggie a home and I never saw her again. I always asked if I could visit her. I never got any information about where she was, or how I could visit her. I never saw her again. I heard her new human guardian got her pregnant and she had puppies. I will always miss the times that we could have had together.

This is a very common situation that happens when you don't own your own home, you are young and living at home with your parents. This may have happened to someone that you know. So please be cautious to look at the long term plan of pet ownership. The people you live with may not be so understanding or patient when it comes to your dogs. People often change their minds and situations can change fast.

What to Consider When Getting a New Pet

Puppy Snowie's Adoption Video!

Most everyone when adopting, wants a puppy thinking that they can handle the dog better when it grows up. This is far from the truth. Dogs require lots of time, a good schedule of feeding, grooming, bath-

room, walking, training, exercise and attention every day.

Puppies grow up very quickly and often get out of control running circles around the owners. There is also the possibility of your pet destroying some of your belongings, as your new dog get acclimated to your home. Bringing in an additional pet could create tension with your existing pets in the household.

Do your due diligence when adopting a dog to take your time and not rush into any quick decisions. Make sure you get a dog that you can walk and is manageable. Dogs all have a different personality that can lead to a dog being returned. It is important to get a behaviorist enhancement dog trainer or staff member that is knowledgable to help you during the process of picking a new addition to your family. They can be extremely helpful in making your decision.

Make Sure you can Have Pet's Where you Live

If you rent or lease your home, make sure you first have permission from your landlord to adopt a pet, especially before falling in love with a dog or cat. Check your lease agreement and reach out to your land lord or owner of the property, to make sure you got approval from them. This is a very common reason dogs get returned. Be sure to bring a letter from your landlord or property manager stating permission to adopt. This can speed up the adoption process and it may be necessary to provide proof of this.

- **About 50% of dogs are returned to shelter after adoption.**

- **20% within the first 2 weeks.**

I have personally witnessed dogs being returned at an adoption event, within 15 minutes, after being adopted at a mega adoption event. A young lady did not consult with her boyfriend and he said he did not like the way the dog looked.

Your Dogs Exercise and Bathroom Needs

Cesar ended up at the same kill shelter about 5 times before getting adopted furever. He always *found a way to get out of his property; by means of digging under, or jumping over high fences. Huskies are known for being great escape artists and need lots of exercise. He was adopted.*

Keep in mind that a secure **fenced in yard** will be needed; if your lifestyle does not include **walking your dog** several times a day. It's most important to make time to take your pet out to go to the bathroom at least 2 times a day for 20-minute walks. This is minimal for some dogs. Some dogs will need more exercise, basic obedience or socializing than others. This depends on their level of energy. Walks provide a great mental and physical workout for you and your dog. By nature, dogs are designed to travel distances in a pack with other dogs. Some dogs may feel confined and trapped looking at the same four walls day in and out for years, therefore can cause, stress and some behavioral issues.

It's been recommended 10 blocks for every ten pounds. Of course, you have to consider the dog's age, breed, size, and overall health. The average time dogs should spend is between 30 minutes to two hours of activity every day.

Letting your dog loose in front of your home property can cause many safety issues for you and your dog Like: running after cats, children, pedestrians, joggers, getting hit by car, getting hurt, nuisance to neighbors or even getting your local animal control service attention. Your dog can be overprotective guarding their home. This can lead to someone or an animal getting bit and or scratched.

This is one of my German Shepherds Joy-Bird. One day I found her at Miami Dade Animal Service after straying from home. She looked so scared. This is us below on a cross-county trip with her half brother Hawkeye in the Grand Canyon. She lived a full life and a was 11 years old when she died of cancer.

Apartment Living Arrangements

This scenario is not ideal for all dogs. Breed limitation has commonly created an issues with neighbors and building associations. Some large dogs are happy to lounge around all day while, some small ones will tear your apartment apart if they don't get to run free for at least twice a day. Barking problems are very common.

Strange noises and people can make a pup anxious and cause him to act out by destroying property, or barking excessively throughout the day. It's important to get them used to their environment by allowing them to interact with people living around you.

- Establish a bathroom relief routine.
- Hire a dog walker, daycare or dog sitter.
- Homeowners have the ability to install a doggie door so the dog can let themselves out to potty.

Tips on Securing Your Property for Your New Pet!

Keep your new pet with you indoors on a leash, until you know your dog won't destroy everything in sight, or in a secured fenced yard. This is so you can spend time getting to know your new pet. Keep in mind, animals are unpredictable and can just run off: after a squirrel, bird or cat and knock you down. You may even have trouble retrieving your dog and that could result in an avoidable dangerous situation.

Make sure your dog cannot jump your fence, and that your yard is secured all-around your property premises before you let them run around lose off the leash. It is very common for some new pets to jump or climb high fences, dig a hole under the fence, open side fences, gates, or door if you don't have a close eye on them. This happens very quickly and it is very common: so caution! Your new pet may not know the **"come"** command (the most important command), their "name", or know you well enough, therefore can result in them running away from you even faster and into traffic!

It is very common when families move into a new home that their dogs find a way to stray. This is because often the new home or property is not doggie proof yet. Dogs can even find a way to open a window by pushing it open from the inside.

.

If you have family or friends visiting, they may not see your dog and this aids your dog to run away from your home; by them leaving a gate or door open, or by just forgetting to close and shut the door.

If your new home is not secured, there is a good chance that your new pet will stray away from home. This is why it is so important to secure your property inside and out before bringing in any new pets. By starting your dog and yourself on some basic training: sit, stay, come, dog limitations, boundaries, potty and crate training, you can count on a healthy and successful relationship to come.

I recommend useing your local resources to get information about group training classes, or private certified dog trainers in your area. This will be an excellent investment of your time and money.

Make Sure You Can Afford and Keep a Safe and Clean Home Environment for Your Dog

This is for both you and your pet's benefit. Dogs track in dirt, feces and anything imaginable in to your home.

You can use a damp cloth to wipe clean paws and or dry them off if they are wet, before coming in, or as soon as they come in your home for the night. If your pet is welcome on furniture you may want to put fresh clean covers over your furniture: to maintain cleanliness. You will need to shake, brush away excess hair and wash them regularly. If you adopt a furry dog, you will have to comb them regularly and do a lot of sweeping. Every time you touch or pet your dog, you could have hair everywhere. Some dogs are sensitive to cleaning chemicals we use that may cause flaking. Keep in mind that dogs have amazing smelling senses. With their high sensitivity, that they can not avoid being around smoke or strong odors.

Kingston - Adopted

Maintenance Expense

Pet ownership requires you to **keep your pet up to date on all vaccinations**. Use good quality food to keep your pet healthy. Always check the nutrition content in the food to ensure that, your dog is getting the proper amount of nutrition. Lack of nutrition can lead to skin conditions. Keep current on vaccines, heartworm medication and annual checkups. Grooming, teeth cleaning maintenance, treats, crates/kennel, leashes, collars, bedding, and toys. Calculate all this realistically, to figure out how much that, will cost you. If you can't afford a dog with a maintenance expense, then consider having an emergency reserve available or available credit to cover for your pet's emergency bill, if you were to have one. *Maintenance medical insurance and emergency medical insurance are available and recommended*. Both will cover your pets, for different needs. Always have a plan of action to provide care for your pet. If anything were to happen, you should be prepared by having your local veterinarian 24-hour emergency animal clinic phone number available.

While getting to know your dog, he or she could run into medical issues. Contact your veterinarian to assess your pet's health issues. ***Try to get a copy of the medical history on your potential new pet.*** Your pet may need medications, surgery or other important treatments.

Unfortunately, this is a very common reason for pet owners to return their new pets back into a shelter. It's very difficult to find a home for a sick or elderly dog with medical issues.

Most cities require *spay/neuter programs* to help cut down on shelter in-take and euthanasia numbers. Sterilizing your furry friend will benefit your pet in many ways; by reducing the risk of cancer, infection, managing temperament and extra energy. It will

also reduce or help stop your dog from straying away from home. This is mandatory in most states.
A fee is charged to maintain a breeder's license to register the dog; if your dog is not sterilized.

Traveling Tips!

When traveling for extended stays in certain cities, there are regulations in place for Breed-Specific Legislation (BSL). Be certain your breed of dog is allowed in the city that you are traveling to.

It is important to have a **travel plan,** especially if you travel often. When you are planning to be away for **long periods of time**, or spend long hours at work, make sure your dog is secure and has food and water. Having someone check in on your dog while you are away is highly recommended. Travel is one of the biggest reasons animal shelters are full during the holidays. People are traveling or relocating and

can't take their animal companions. It is important to have a plan because your pet counts on you. There are pet-friendly hotels in many cities.

Leo - ID # A1729076

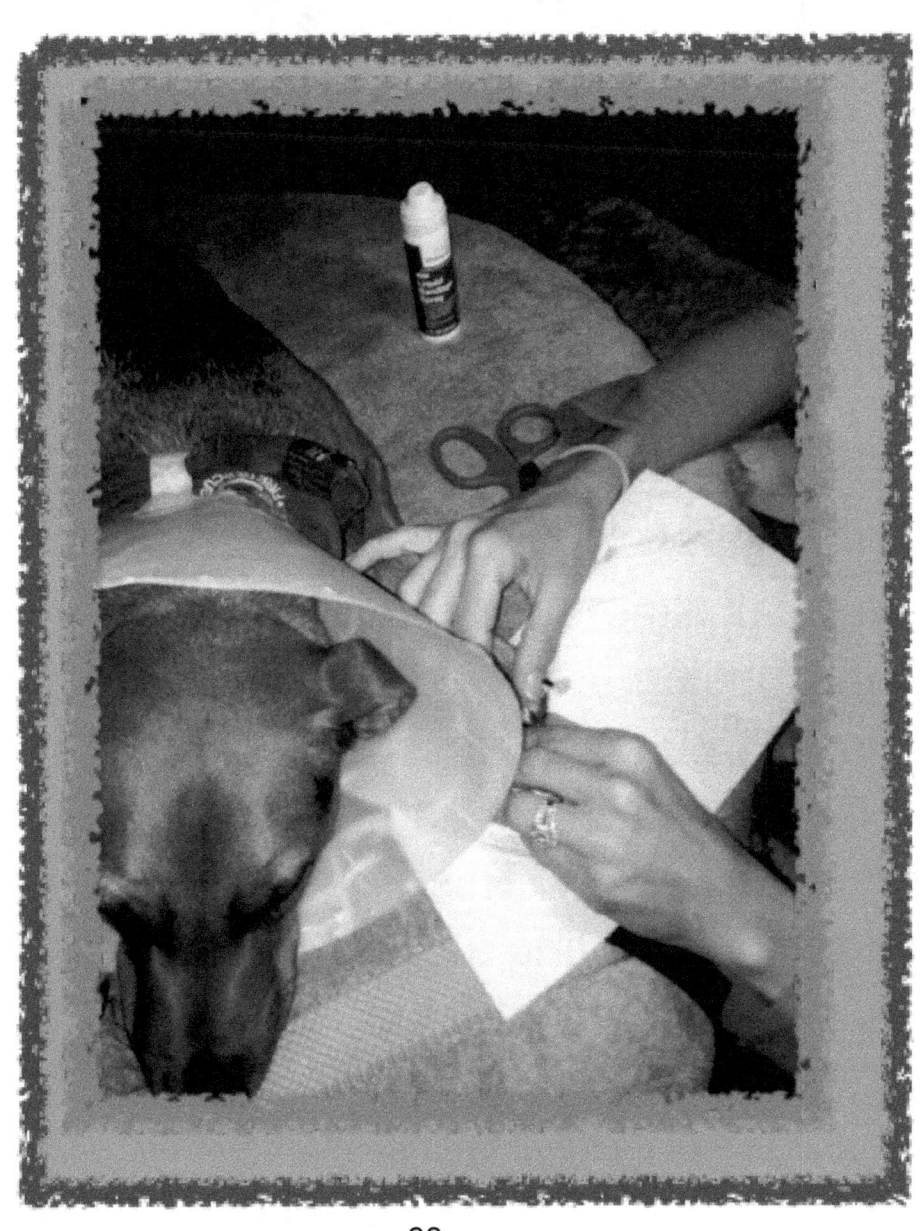

First Aid Kit

In case of an emergency with your dog or someone else's dog; being prepared will help you get through this. Having quick to access your first aid kit, followed by quick thinking, is necessary to handle any emergency situation. This is going to be a very important factor in saving a dog's life.

Keep your pet's first aid kit in your car and take it with you when traveling. To start your first aid kit, you can buy a first-aid kit designed for people and add pet-specific items to it. You can also purchase a pet first-aid kit from a pet supply store or online. You can easily assemble your own kit by gathering items like these:

- Dog leash, water, disinfectant, cotton balls, gauze tape, scissors which will assist you if you come across any injured dog and/or cat.

- **Blankets and towels** can be used to lay over the dog or cat to create protection, safety for the animal and yourself. It is a great asset for moving the injured animal as well as when transporting an animal to an emergency clinic.

- Phone numbers to your veterinarian, or the nearest emergency veterinary clinic are a must: Be prepared!

- Pet's medical records should be stored in a waterproof container or bag. Proof of rabies vaccination status, copies of other important medical records and have a current photo of your pet in case they are lost. Please ensure all animals are microchipped for scanning identification that reads your current information correctly. Also, occasionally get tested it to ensure your information pulls up correctly, with a backup number to a relative or close friend. If you have changed your phone number or moved from your registered address, just make sure you update it within a month.

•Muzzle or strips of cloth to prevent biting (don't use this if the animal is vomiting because it can cause choking).

•Self-cling bandage (this will not stick to fur)

Chapter 3
Different Dog Breeds Shelter Stories

Blue's True Story

Blue's Adoption Video

At first sight, you may get the impulse to adopt a dog as beautiful and stunning as Blue. He was adopted out to an adopter that signed an agreement to give him back to the rescue, if they were not happy with keeping him, which is common for rescues to do. I knew the person that adopted him. I had offered to help when they had complained to me about: his high energy, he was getting ticks, his fur hair was hard for them to keep up their home and yard clean.

One day the owner handed Blue over to a stranger at the animal control (kill shelter) parking lot. Those people then gave Blue to someone else. He then ended up at a small dog rescue. It took about 7 months of him getting bounced around, till he was found stray again and was scanned with animal control. The registered rescue on his microchip was called and assumed responsibility. Blue was in bad shape, both physically and emotionally.

I spend the next few months trying to get him adopted again. The family that originally adopted him is now registered on a National Do Not Adopt List. Happy dance for Blue on getting successfully adopted!

Coda

Coda had a severe case of Demodex; no hair, in pain, red and irritated. He was treated with IV's at Jupiter Animal Hospital. In this picture, he has some new hair growth! GTS Husky Rescue.

Lucky

This Husky had his eye removed, then lost his vision in the other eye. This was because his previous owner did not give him eye drops. He was in a lot of pain. As soon as he had his surgery, he had a smile back on his face. He got adopted to a volunteer. GTS Husky Rescue.

Dizzy

Born totally blind, This pit bull brindle mix was an owner surrender to shelter. He was adopted! He looked like he was always looking at me.

Ice Cream

Ice Cream's Adoption Video!

She was run over by a car and she was in a lot of pain. She got adopted, returned and then got adopted again!

Icee

Shelter Dogs from Palm Beach County Animal Care & Control

Vonda's Adoption Video!

Vonda was found with severe Demodex; no hair on her body and in a lot of pain. She was rescued and adopted!

Ghoast's Adoption Video!

Ester

On 4/20/14, I took this amazing picture! She is a very large-framed female, 100 lbs. She was playing in the kennel with another dog. They ran and played like crazy.

Beisha

This beautiful 10 years old, German Shepherd ended up at the shelter because her owner went into assisted living facility and could not find anyone to take her. Beisha spent several months at the shelter with many other kennel dog mates before she got adopted. She was returned the next day because she wanted to say hello to another dog and the new owner could not manage her well. She got back on the adoption floor after a week on hold in quarantine. She then got adopted a couple of weeks after.

When I took her out she would always look for her owner.

Sandy's Adoption Video!

Senior Sandy 11 years old, white German Shepherd; was taken to a rescue during a hurricane and her owner never came back. She is good with cats, but unfortunately not with other dogs. It took about 2

years to get her adopted. During that time she was confined to a kennel most all day and was only hand walked.

Rodger Dodger's Special Adoption Video!

This is Rodger Dodger my foster failure after being returned several times. He developed severe anxiety after spinning in circles for 6 months at the shelter. He lost his bottom 3 front teeth from biting on the kennel rods and was heartworm positive. I later found out he was shot 2 times and still had the gun pellets in him.

Coco Bean Adoption Video!

Stella's Story Video!

Chapter 4
Tips for Children with Dogs

All children need supervision and special attention when being introduced to new animals. They should *never* be left alone with dogs, nor approach any dogs while the dog is *eating, sleeping, guarding (around food or bowls), trash, puppies, toys or while being tethered.*

- Dogs protect their home properties and owner.

- Animals are not toys. I say this with high regard and caution. Please teach your child to treat your pet respectfully. Quite often, children have hurt a dog and/or dogs, and then the dog ends up in a shelter. It's extremely important to *take the time to*

correct the child's behavior immediately after an incident. Proper introduction and training with your dog and family members can lead to a long-time successful and rewarding experience.

- *Children should be taught never to scream, bark, swing objects or run away from a dog because dog are reactive. They can be frightened by them and they should never approach a stray dog.* These are common reactions from children who get excited when seeing a dog, especially if they are not use to being around dogs.

- Children running can trigger a dog to run after them, as dogs are usually faster.

- Avoid and use extra caution around a stray animal. Reach out to anyone around for help, that maybe be familiar with the dog to get him or her back home to safety. Extra caution should be used and do not approach a dog that is not friendly. Children should avoid all lose dogs.

- Children should be taught to **always ask the dog owner's permission** to approach, touch or get close to their dog. Once you have permission, start by offering to let the dog smell **your closed hand, palm/hand calmly face down.**

- He or she will let you know if they want you to pet them. Proceed to pet by going under the neck area. Never go to pet over their heads, unless you are familiar with the dog. They may feel overpowered or scared because they are not familiar with you.

- **Never scare a sleeping dog.** Make a noise first, or say their name softly. Don't approach a dog that is eating. They will defend what they believe is their property.

- **Don't run from a dog.** The chase instinct is very strong in dogs. Walk away slowly. You should walk backwards and do not turn your back until the dog has lost interest.

- Don't try to pet a dog by sticking your hand through a fence or into a crate. The dog may see this as an intrusion into their territory.

- Every dog has the potential to bite a human. Any canine that is threatened, an unfamiliar person or situation, hurt or scared can become a dangerous dog situation.

- Properly training, socializing your pet, educating your children on how to approach and interact with a dog; can help avoid dog bites. By investing some time with your dog with basic training and making sure that your dog walks well (by not pulling when

you walk your dog outside your property and not barking or attacking other animals or people). This way you can avoid future potential seriously dangerous situations. Having a plan is important.

- Use supervision with your child and other pet at all times. Anything can happen. Keep them in separate rooms when you are gone.

- Children must never try to take a toy from a dog's mouth.

- **Children can act out internal issues that parents are not aware of with an animal.** Situations like this can get out of control very quickly. Many times the dog is left frightened, hurt and *traumatized.*

- ***Interacting with animals should always be supervised.*** Investing in your dog with one-on-one

time and training will also teach your child how to

interact with your dog. You may teach them training tricks; by allowing them to give commands to your dog. It's also a great way to spend time together. You will know when your child becomes "a good leader of the pack!"

- ***If a dog can smell a child without feeling threatened, they will usually walk away and leave them alone.*** Teach children proper behavior with dogs. Use caution and do not approach loose animals or injured pets. Encourage your children to notify you if they see any loose or injured dogs. By doing the right thing and contacting the proper au-

thorities, other animals can be saved and/or returned to their original family.

- Teach your children to be ***gentle, caring, compassionate, patient, understanding with your family dog,*** and how not so different they are from us. Our pets depend on us and we need to take care of them. Ensure that your children understand that your pet is a trustworthy friend and to always take care of them.

This is Luna, One of my 9 fosters that was returned because it did not go well with a toddler in the first family that adopted her was too aggressive. It took me another 3 months to find her an awesome furever home!

I'm featuring my neighbor's children interacting properly with their adopted dog, Gracie. She was adopted from Palm Beach County Animal Control at about 5 months old. When the family went to adopt a dog, they walked by Gracie's kennel and she just started howling for them to come back and they adopted her. They felt it was a sure sign that Gracie had chosen them to adopt her!

Chapter 5
How to Introduce Your New Dog to Your Home and Other Pets

Congratulations on your new pet! Welcome to the world of doggie ownership! I'm very excited about the love and beautiful moments you will have with your new best friend and family member for the years to come.

It is important to understand your life will change from this point forward. I encourage you to do your due diligence when choosing your new pet so that you will find a perfect match for your family's lifestyle and personalities and you both develop a lasting relationship. By recognizing breed differences, you will get a better idea of whether or not a dog is right for you. This is important, as you will be living with your new pet for many years to come. So let's get started on the right paw!

How to Get Ready for Your "New Dog" to Come Into Your Home

Before bringing your new pet to your home, you should make sure your home is pet safe. Please take notice of everything and consider for your pet's safety. Get down on all fours to see at your dog's level. Including; looking under and behind beds, tables, and furniture. Look to see what you may notice that your pet could eat or swallow. Things such as paperclips, glass, and metal can be dangerous to your pet and cause choking.

- Your dog may eat personal items like; cell phones, remote controls, furniture, pillows or shoes and any valuables. Watch for electrical and cell phone charger cables and electrical outlets.

- You cannot leave anything to chance. It's not the dog's fault if something gets eaten or destroyed. It's your fault for leaving valuables out for them to eat and destroyed. This could create more bad behaviors. Dogs need supervision. Dogs need you to spend time to teach them what they can play with and what they can not. Keeping a close eye on your new pet will also help to train them. It's in their nature to want to play with everything, so clean your home from top to bottom.

- Put everything of value in storage containers. Establish where your new pet's room, crate, kennel, or playpen will be.

- Installing a *baby gate* in a favorite room might be something long term to think about. The gate installed creates a safe room for your dog like; in the kitchen.

- Make sure you have food and freshwater bowls ready for use with good nutritional food. Larger dogs need their water bowl placed up higher for ingestion. Make sure to properly clean and fill with fresh water every day.

- ***A nice comfortable bed, treats, hair comb and safe toys are encouraged.* Avoid giving rawhide treats because they can be dangerously fatal.**

- Buying **poop bags** and having them handy is something you need to become used to having with you and using.

- I can't stress enough how important it is to have an emergency medical plan. Research different kinds of insurance options for your new pet.

Get familiar with **"*internal parasites*"** such as; roundworm, whipworms, tapeworms, Coccidia and Giardia, that are all health risks to your pet. They can be very painful and life-threatening to your pet. To prevent these common infections, please practice preventative maintenance. Get your pet on heart-worm prevention, as soon as possible. Practice good hygiene.

How to Doggie Proof Your Home Inside and Outside!

A **fenced-in yard** is a bonus for a dog owner. The fence should be buried into the ground, giving no outlet or escape route to your dog. It should be high enough for a dog not to be able to jump over easily.

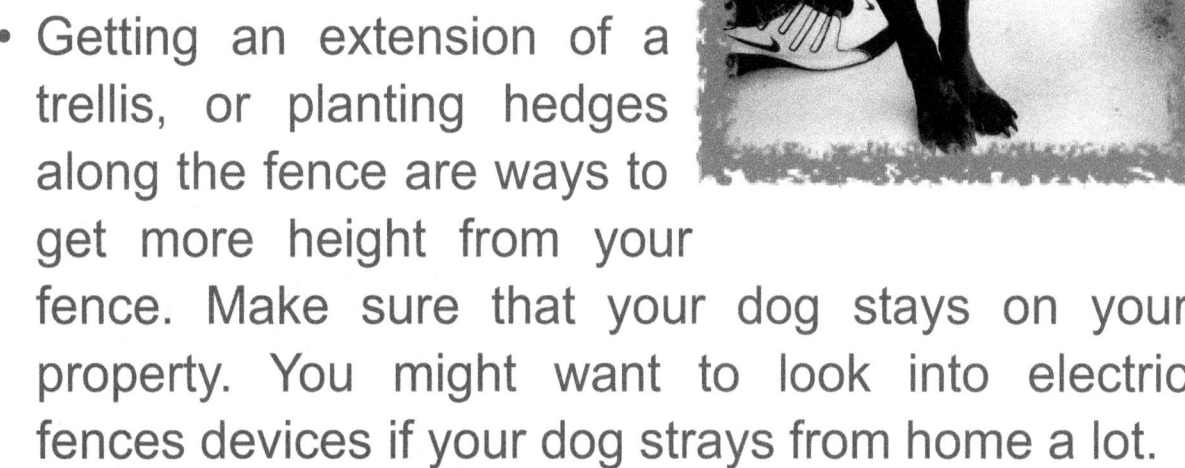

- Getting an extension of a trellis, or planting hedges along the fence are ways to get more height from your fence. Make sure that your dog stays on your property. You might want to look into electric fences devices if your dog strays from home a lot.

- Make sure all **gates and doors** coming in and out of your property can be easily be securely **closed, so dogs can not open them.** It is very common for dogs to roam off the property and cause other problems with neighbors (to say the least).

- Use **extra caution** when you have workers or friends visiting your home, and make sure they always *remember to close doors behind them.* Dogs may stray and many things can go wrong for your pet.

- **Always know exactly where all your pets are,** especially when cars are driving in and out of your property. Dogs like to sneak out because, they are very curious and like to explore. I cannot express enough how important security is for your pet on your property so that they do not get run over by cars on your property.

This is one of my pedigree German Shepherds that was given to me as an engagement present. At about 4-5 months old. He was run over by a car on my property when I was out of town. May he RIP.

Pools Safety

Supervise your new dog when near a pool. Some dogs are excellent natural swimmers while others are not. Always make sure your pet knows how to get out of the pool, in case they fall in. Dogs can get serious diseases by going in a poorly maintain pool, dirty water or even the beach. (Check out more details in my other Everything Dogs Book, "Dog's Emergencies - Common Pet Emergency").

First Car Ride Safety

Most dogs love car rides, but for some it may be a little too much! So let's make the drive home is as safe as possible. Often dogs will jump out, can be lodged in the event of an accident from a sharp turn. Pet guardian fail to trust that dogs are safe, when they are not, resulting in very commonly getting killed by moving vehicles. Dogs also commonly get run over on their own property. So always caution!

Here are some tips:

- Keep your doggie on a leash. Leash laws are enforced in many other areas. Do not let your pet off the leash during transit or in public, no matter what!

- During your car ride keep music and voices to a low level. Dogs' ears are very sensitive. High pitched voices can make a dog very nervous. You and your dog should be in a calm state on your drive. Act normal. Animals have an extreme sense of smell with their nose; that can give them information about you. No need to overpower them with strong perfume or smoke. They are also great

observers and will read what your body language is saying. You should do the same and watch them closely, so you too can learn about them. Animals feed on your energy. A good calm and assertive energy is the kind of energy you will want to maintain.

- Windows should be up or only slightly open, so that your new pet does not jump out.

- Make sure your dog can not open the door or windows

throughout your vehicle. To avoid them popping a door open.

- You may want to bring a crate to transport your new pet safely home.

- ***An unsecured 60-pound dog traveling at 35 miles per hour can turn into a 2,700 pound projectile in a car accident.*** Keep your dog safe with the right travel harness and attach it to a seat harness; one without tethers. This allows your pet to sit and lay down.

- According to American Humane, 100,000 **dogs** are **killed** each year in accidents involving riding in **truck** beds. Veterinarians say they see numerous cases of **dogs** injuring themselves by jumping out; breaking legs and joint injuries. This often results in amputation or in hanging themselves, or even being run over. Dogs may see something and want to go after it in traffic because they are reactive by nature. In case you are in a car accident or have to break or stop suddenly, your dog would be a shooting projectile.

What to do When You Get Home with Your New Pet

Dogs need time to adjust to new their new environment. Your house is a strange new place   for your new pet! All they need is a little time to realize they are now in a safe loving home.

- ***Show him/her where the designated new pet area is*** and let them relax there for a bit. Let them smell and decompress a bit and get familiar with where their place is. Show them that, they belong and that this is their "new room". If you have a kennel crate in there, you can later teach your dog: "go to your house" or "go to your room".

- Show **your new pet their food, water, bed, and toys.**

- **Watch** and try to avoid them from destroying any toys or bedding. When your dog tries to eat something he/she is not supposed to, just put it away for a while. Then reintroduce the item on another day to train them on what they can and cannot eat, or destroy. Showing or giving them a toy, that they can play with when this happens, will immediately *redirect* your dog to learn to play with the right toys.

- If you have other pets, give your **new doggie his own safe room.** Keep the door closed and keep the other pets out. Don't worry, you will introduce them later. Give new doggie time to figure out where they can feel safe, until they get acclimated to everyone. This also allows for your existing pets to get adjusted to your new dog. but most importantly establishes *boundaries, limitations, and placement.*

- Act normal and make sure you *give all dogs equal time and attention.* Do not leave new pets unsupervised.

- When you take your new dog outside to use the bathroom, **keep him/her on a leash and away from your other pets.**

- **Make sure your new dog is going to the bathroom** and check his/her stool. Sometimes it takes a few days for your new dog to settle down. It can take a while for your new dog to feel comfortable or safe to go to the bathroom in an unfamiliar place without them thinking they may get into trouble.

- In the beginning, **walk your pet on leash on your property to help him/her become familiar.** They gather information by sniffing around. By doing this, your pet can learn a lot. Gradually you can give your dog more freedom by dropping the leash on the ground. This way your dog will recognize that you are still watching over him/her and controlling still in control of the situation. You are guiding them to do what you want them to do; like going to the bathroom unleashed in the yard. Your dog will learn what you are going to be doing next and will eagerly await the next command.

- Dog *love and need routines and need a schedule.* Dogs only want to make you happy. They want you to tell them what you want them to do next. Your new pets may not have been trained with any commands before. This is when teaching your dog the *"come command"* can be a good time. Always use your leash with your dog when you take your dog anywhere.

- *Training your dog to sit, lay down, stay and come, will make entering and exiting your home, or going to play in the yard a pleasant experience.* It teaches them to pay attention to you. Especially for dogs that like to jump and run

off because, of their natural tendencies. If your dog does not respond well to your commands, it can lead to other bad behavior. It is advisable to teach them to watch you for commands. Having treats in you pocket can be very helpful. You should be able to control and train your dog from the very beginning. As to having problems, developing a bad behavior with your dog by not listening to you; makes the repeated correction more difficult and longer for your dog to catch on.

- Dogs' laws of nature require three things in this order: **Exercise, obedience, and love:** which equal rewards.

- **You should take your dog for walking exercises and bathroom breaks every day**. It is good for your pet's mind and body. This is a great way to know that your pet is going to the bathroom regularly.

- ***Dogs learn by repetition and with a rewards system.*** It is a good idea to run through some basic commands, before you take your pet out for a walk, or to take them anywhere. This so you can handle your dog from jumping, barking at other dogs, or embarrassing moments your dogs that, can cause you safety issues. Some dogs may need to go to the bathroom more than others. Again, a good guide for how much exercise your dog needs is two street blocks for every 10 pounds of their body weight. Puppies can hold an hour, for every month they are in age. Of course, this varies.

- **Fast movement, can scare a dog or may cause the dog to want to run away or react.** When you have your dog on leash; please use caution when approaching other dogs, cats, possums, children running, bouncing balls, bicycles, skateboards, fireworks, and thunder and lightning.

- You should always have your pet first on a **complete "sit and stay" before you give them any food reward and have them remain in stay**, until you tell them it's "okay" to "come" out of the command and then play, or praise.

- Introducing your new pet to your family and other pets is extremely important. **Remember that your new pet is amongst strangers and will need time to adjust to his or her new life and environment.**

Chapter 6
Introducing Your New Dog to Your Existing Pets!

- By taking dogs out for a walk and to play first, it can help your fur-chid to let go of some excess energy. This is so that they can be better focused on your direction.

- Your existing doggie or other pets are less likely to view this new doggie as an intruder if their first meeting takes place in a neutral location, or you can arrange for a meet and greet at the shelter or rescue with your existing dogs. A new park is highly recommended for introductions.

- Each dog should be handled by a different person or holder.

- Calmly start to walk alongside each dog. Over time, walk dogs along to merge to end up together. If your dog is pulling while walking, stop. You must be in control of your dog before you continue to walk. This will teach your dog to look to you for the next command. Keeping some yummy doggie treats in a hip pouch, pocket or hand to get you started with one dog only (but do not use treats, food or toys right away with pairing new dogs together). Only so you can get their attention and have them ready to "sit and stay", instead of pulling you. This can be very helpful. Let them smell your hand, so they know you got treats to reward him or her for their good behavior. **A plastic bottle with pennies can be used as a corrector or even a light water spray bottle.** Your dog's shoulders should be back and down with no tension on the leash while on a complete stop. Before you continue, make sure you can handle your pet calmly and assertively.

- Dogs say hello by sniffing. So let them say hello, but only briefly and manageable. Never put dogs face to face. Side by side is safer. Avid dogs locking on tunnel vision with each others, so you can keep it under control before it can escalate. This way they can safely smell each others personal areas. When this happens they are exchanging information about each other, and getting to know one another. **Keep them separate, until you can casually get them walking side by side together.**

- Walk the dogs and let them explore the area. Allow them to interact with each other, on and off the leash while verbal praised, encouraged and using treats at this point. Do not introduce toys or treats right away.

- **Use caution during meals and treat times,** by separating your pets. Feed your dogs separately in their room, kennel or designated area.

- Watch your new dog behavior and always make eye contact. This will teach you a lot about your dog!

- The **"play-bow"** posture is when your dog puts his front legs on the ground and his hind end up in the air. This is an **invitation** to play and is a good opportunity for another dog to come sniff them.

- **Caution signs with your pets includes;** hair standing up on the dog's back, showing their teeth, deep growling, long , and a stiff-legged posture. If these occur, separate the dogs. Also, you can be distracting them by having them do a trick and then give them a treat away from the other dog. You don't want the other dog to think he is getting special treatment so they both may need a treat. Start the introduction process again. Move more slowly this time. Your pets may need to have a timeout from the situation before you try again.

- If you have more than one dog, *repeat* **this process of introduction with each pet.** Separately, one on one, so they won't gang up on the new doggie. They can all get equal time of getting use to each others smells and personalities. If a dog does not want to interact with your new addition, do not force it. It will come with time. Sometimes dogs can have dog aggression toward other dogs, because they never had socialization skills with other dogs proper introduction or are just older.

- Meeting other pets should be a slow process and should be spread out over a few days, weeks, months or even longer, if necessary. **Always use caution** and remember to always spend equal time with each dog.

- Many older dogs will be upset, jealous, or even angry with a new puppy. Especially, if the older dog has been an only dog. It's going to be important to make sure the older dog gets a lot more than normal attention to alleviate any potential hurt feelings.

- ***It is very crucial to intervene if your new puppy / younger dog is tormenting your older dog*** or existing pet; to avoid your puppy from getting bit. Older dogs do not have the same energy nor mindset. They may be suffering from muscular pain that, you may not know about. A strange new dog that just popped up out of nowhere can make them defensive or jealous and can develop issues later.

- *Two alpha females can get along just fine if the owners are true leaders.* They may fight if the owners are not. On the other hand, even two submissive follower type females can begin to fight, if the humans are weak pack leaders.

Resource Guarding

A dog might have a resource guarding issues with items like; a favorite toy, ball, a bowl of kibbles, or a soft spot on the sofa. Dogs can be possessive. Past traumas, genetics and the competition of having multiple pets can cause an issue.

Older dogs may be more sensitive to tolerating a new dog: so use caution!

If your **dog** growls, lunges or shows other obvious **guarding** behavior, you are too close.

Common Signs of Resource Guarding

- Growling while eating.
- Defending bones, other treats or toys.
- Snapping, biting and growling if you get close to their food bowl.
- Dog guarding food, but not eating.
- Attacking or growling at other dogs during mealtime.
- Eating much faster, when someone is near.

Resource Guarding Tips

You may need a professional to help you and your furry companion.

1. Use treats as positive reinforcement.
2. Focus on desensitization.
3. Avoid punishment.
4. Teach your dog to share.
5. Pet them during meals.
6. Solving food aggression between the dogs.

Questions or Concerns - If you are worried about your dog and feel that, they are not adjusting properly, please contact the organization you adopted your dog from. They can hopefully give you the proper guidance in offering you advice or training. It can just be something very simple. We want you and your dog to have a happy long life together with you and your all your family members!

Tips for Introducing Your New Dog to Your Cat!

Before they meet face to face, let your cat and dog meet nose to nose, I recommend getting to know each other by allowing them to get familiar with each other's pets' scent. For instance, take doggie's bedding from his room and allow your cat to smell it. Take kitty's bedding and allow your dog to smell it. Letting the dogs see and smell your kitty's litter is also a good idea.

Next time let them see each other. You can use a baby gate to separate them, or a doorstop to crack the door a few inches. If you have multiple pets, do this with each one at a time. Watch closely and cautiously.

Now let's try real contact. Keep doggie on a good leash and allow cat to approach him.

- **Speak softly to both pets and cautiously give them treats.** Keep your eyes on both of them, so that you can remain in control. I would not encourage you to do this for a long time. Your relationship and obedience should not always consist of food reward. It should be praise. Once your dogs understand commands like: "stop, no, stay and sit".

- ***No sudden or fast movement*** because it can frighten them.

- ***If your pets hiss or growl, this is normal.*** It means they are communicating. Fighting is not normal and should be avoided at all costs.

- ***Keep a close eye on these interactions.*** Even if your pets likes other animals, every situation is unique. You never know what could happen. So watch very closely and keep alert to assure safety to your pets and yourself.

- ***Meeting other pets should be a slow process and spread out over a few days or longer.*** It can sometimes take a month or even longer. Some dogs may have dog aggression with other dogs and towards cats. If that is the case, the sooner you get a good reputable dog trainer, the better. You don't want to send the wrong message to your dogs or getting them use to bad habits that, can cause you more issues later on.

Introducing Your New Dog to Your Chicken

Give your dog plenty of exercise before introduction to your chicken(s). Before the introduction, take your dog running, swimming, playing catch or an extra long walk to help tire your dog out and spend extra-time with them. This will help prepare your dog's frame of mind.

Check out my "Juno" sharing his breakfast with his sweet chicken family members; "Lupita and Juanita".

- First, feed your dog and give them water.

- Make sure your chickens are secured in their coop and that there is no way for your chickens to get out or your dog getting to them. You will need a **good collar and short leash for optimal** control of your dog to keep your chickens safe.

Walk around the chicken coop and note their reactions to one another. Notice how your chicken behaves. If you have any aggression or growling from your dog, take them away immediately. Only reward and praise your dog, if they do well. Try this again every day at the same time, or even twice a day after breakfast and dinner.

Two Person Introduction

- This is when one person holds the chicken and the other person has good control of a well-behaved dog. Then you can allow your dog to smell your chicken. If it goes well, again praise and treats. If your dog growls or barks; walk away. You may need help from a trainer, or it could take a while. Hopefully, over time, they will start getting use to each other and it will work out.

- Never leave dogs unattended with the chickens. Keep your coop secured. If you work on your yard or garden and your chicken(s) are o, simply keep your dog on a leash with you, till you see that your dog is not interested in your chicken.

- You can train your dog with treats, to back off with commands like; "off, leave it, or take it" for treats.

- Temporary, you may want to muzzle only for training. Always use extra caution to keep your chicken(s) safe. Dogs may run after your chickens, so reconsider fostering dogs, or dog sitting for other people. It is common for chickens to get killed by dogs because, it is instinctual for dogs to be reactive to a movement for some dogs more than others.

Chewing House Training

Dogs always need guidance from us. They are natural pleasers and want to make you happy! Help your dog understand what you want from them with these simple tips.

Puppies Destroying a Pillow Video!

Give doggie plenty of dog toys. For example, don't give your new pet old shoes or socks to play with. Reinforce positive behaviors with healthy natural treats, instead of your personal belongings. Keep your belongings out of your doggie's reach. Put away items of value, such as; shoes, clothes and remote controls. *It's important to catch your pet in action when chewing on something that he that, they are not suppose to chew on.*

- **Keeping a leash on your pet at all times** when you first bring them in to your home will help prevent any unplanned incidents. You will need to keep a close leash on your new pet. Meaning putting a leash on your dog and have your dog attached to you. Introducing them to a new home properly from the start will be very beneficial! The younger the dog, or if it's a puppy, the longer your new pet can take to adapt. Accidents happen very quickly. Your pet is probably going to snatch something you don't want them to. This is because, dogs need a lot of attention, exercise and very curious. Even while you are in the same room, just looking in the other direction, your dog can destroy many things. You will be surprised! It is important to make corrections and redirect your dog to a proper chewing toy and their "placement" (crate, room, spot or bed), "for a time out".

- **If you catch your pet chewing** on something they should not be, immediately say, "NO" to interrupt them and/or clap your hands. Offer them one of their toys and when they take it, give them lots of praise.

- **Play with him or her!** Dogs often chew when they are bored. Playing with them with their toys and using positive enforcement. It will help your doggie understand what is "okay" for them to chew on. You may want to add some peanut butter to treat, and interest them in it!

- **Don't use punishment.** Once doggie has chewed or went to the bathroom up something, it's too late. Even if it occurred only a few minutes ago, he or she won't understand why you are upset. Instead, **praise him** heavily when he is doing the **RIGHT** thing! Showing in them the right place to go to the bathroom is encouraged as soon as you bring them home from the shelter, and getting them on a schedule.

- Apply a common commercial dog chewing spray. You can also make your own, by combining two parts apple cider vinegar with one part regular white vinegar. You can also try combining bitter apple, with a touch of cayenne pepper, aloe vera gel, or hot sauce in a spray bottle. Shake well and then apply it on the furniture, or on the items that your dog likes to chew on to stops your dogs from chewing on them. The smell will deter them.

- Most importantly, remove whatever your pet is chewing on from every room. Then re-introduce it a week later, or wait longer. This helps to reprogram your dog, but watch his behavior when you bring the item back into reintroducing it. You can let him know you got your eye on him or her and be prepared to catch your dog before he goes for it again.

Chapter 7
Leaving Dogs Home Alone

Crate Training

When you plan on leaving your pets home alone it is a great time for crate training. It becomes a positive safe experience for your pet. Make sure your dog is safe. That they can't play with anything dangerous that can cause choking. Keep them away from all other pets. Most importantly, remove the dog's collar when you leave them alone.

- ***Don't leave your pets together unattended.*** Separate them when you leave the house. Unless you have had them for a very long time and you are 100 percent certain that there won't be a situation while you are gone. Keep in mind that all animals are unpredictable!

- ***Never leave anything to chance because dogs are mischievous.*** They could fight and cause a bad situation while you are gone, and no one will be there to stop them. It can happen just by someone walking by your home and your dogs can get competitive for some other reason like: *resources guarding behavior*. They could also feed from each other's puppy energy and have a little party while you are away by potentially destroying your couch, pillow, walls or wood furnishings. Everything you thought was safe for them to be around is not. They can even set your house on fire.

- Careful with running dogs, tripping and glass furnisher or objects. You could trip over or onto them. You and your dogs could also get cut.

Putting Belonging Away

I can not mention this enough, put everything away (in a safe place) that, you would not want your new pet to eat or that you do not want to have to replace. Especially, anything that can he/she could choke on. This is very common. It's very important to teach your pet limitations, boundaries and respect of your property: right away! Animals are smarter than people think, but they learn even more quickly with positive reinforcement. Please be patient with your dog.

- Choose **toys** that are the right size for your dog. Giving a small toy to a large dog poses a risk of inhalation and choking. Small balls are especially dangerous, as they can easily become lodged in your dog's trachea and be hard to remove.

- Generally speaking, you should choose large toys for large dogs and smaller toys only for smaller dogs.

- Avoid toys with small parts that can be chewed or pulled off and swallowed.
- *Avoid toys with sharp edges, or that can be chewed into sharp points*.

- **Be careful about letting your dog play with sticks.** Avoid sticks that have sharp ends and choose one that, is not too long or too short for your dog to be able jab it into the ground when carried vertically (like a straw), as this could impale your dog's mouth.

- When playing fetch, **avoid toys that are overly heavy or hard.** This might damage your pet's teeth or injure him.

- **If your dog likes to de-stuff toys,** be sure they are not eating the stuffing. Some dogs enjoy stuffing-free toys, which you can purchase skin only, or make one yourself by removing the fluff.Going for Walks

Going for Walks

If you are leaving home, walk; your dog first. Bathroom breaks and fresh air is very beneficial. This will also help keep your pet from having ***separation anxiety. Whining and barking are symptoms.***

This can be a nuisance and may annoy your neighbors. In which case, you may want to make sure your dog gets plenty of exercise before you leave home. Always make sure to leave food and water for your pet.

- ***Their bladder needs to be emptied every hour for every month of age.*** So, a two-month-old puppy needs to use the bathroom every two hours. Consider getting the help of a family member or dog walker, if you can not be home for most of the day.

- ***Establish a routine.*** Doggies will do best when there are certain times that, they eat, play and go outside to potty. For example; take doggies outside after every meal.

- Crate training can help with proper guidance and keeping them safe.

- ***Do not use punishment.*** Once your dog has had an accident, it's too late. Even if it only occurred a few minutes ago, they will not understand why you are upset. They may become too afraid to use the bathroom in your presence. Instead, praise them heavily when he goes to the ***right*** place. Puppies will especially need very frequent potty breaks.

- The afternoon is a great time to give your dog a treat. Get them to sit first and maybe have them give you their paw. Watch for behaviors that your dog may be telling you that indicate they need to go to the bathroom.

Dog Collar Caution

Take collar on your dog off when you leave them in the crate/kennel, so that, they do not choke themselves. Make sure it is safe and that they can not

push themselves out and get hurt. It is very common for dogs to die from a collar strangulation.

Toy Precautions

- Choose *toys* that are the right size for your dog. Giving a small toy to a large dog poses a risk of inhalation and choking. Small balls are especially dangerous, as they can easily become lodged in your dog's trachea and be hard to remove.

- Generally speaking, you should choose large toys for large dogs and smaller toys only for smaller dogs.

- Avoid toys with small parts that can be chewed or pulled off and swallowed.

- Avoid toys with sharp edges, or that can be chewed into sharp points.

- Be careful about letting your dog play with sticks. Avoid sticks that have sharp ends and choose one that, is not too long or too short for your dog to be able jab it into the ground when carried vertically (like a straw), as this could impale your dog's mouth.

- When playing fetch, avoid toys that are overly heavy or hard. This might damage your pet's teeth or injure him.

- Again, if your dog likes to de-stuff toys, be sure they are not eating the stuffing. Some dogs enjoy stuffing-free toys, which you can purchase skin only, or make one yourself by removing the fluff.

Toys and Treats You Shouldn't Leave Your Alone Pet With

Dogs should not play with strings, ribbons, pantyhose, socks or rubber bands. These objects could be swallowed and can cause life-threatening complications once in the digestive tract.

Do not leave your dog alone with rawhide treats because they could kill them by toxic chemicals, It can also cause the dog's stomach to turn, twist and could even lead to death.

Do not give your dog children's toys because they are not designed for dogs.

This is my "Hawk Eye". He died in my jeep as a result of the rawhide twisting in his stomach; in my attempt to rush him to my veterinarian. I felt helpless! More details of rawhide dangers are available in my other; The Everything Dogs Book: "Dogs 911 Emergencies". RIP Hawkeye!

How to Avoid Bathroom Accidents

This is easily done by immediately setting a daily bathroom schedule for your new pet. A good schedule is one that makes your dog the happiest. A natural schedule for a dog, for example: 7:00 a.m. - 7:30 a.m. brisk walk, 7:30 a.m. - 8:00 a.m. eat, then

8:00 a.m. - 9:00 a.m. is a great, opportunity to walk your pet again to potty before you head off to work. So when you get back home, your dogs will be well-rested and properly napped, while you are away. Your pet should be content until lunchtime or when you finally get back home. Over time you will be able to increase the length of time that you are gone.  Use this same bathroom ritual later in the evening around dinner and their playtime. At the same time every day; works best. Your dog will be counting on you from now on to rely on their new schedule. If your dog has healthy bowel movements, then you have a healthy pet.

For puppies; they need to be fed every two hours, and empty their bladder one hour for every month of age. So, a two-month-old puppy will need to go to the bathroom every two hours.

Home Alone Pet Ideas

- You can also install, on an extra old used phone or iPad as a pet monitoring camera. so you can even speak to your dogs from work, or while you are gone to see what they are up to.

- *Lavender* aromatherapy.
- *Relaxing music* or soft TV - I like to leave my dogs with a spa, calming, sleeping, chakra healing music station for them to listen to.

- Online Pet Monitoring System

- Bark Box

- Pet TV Channel

- Pet Treat Dispenser set up to your cell phone

- CBD treats or tincture before you leave for anxious dogs.

Chapter 8
Basic Dog Training
Rewards, Collars, Sit, Come, Place, Lay Down, Praise, Leash Training, Paws Up, Roll Over and more!

Placement

First thing you should do on arriving home is to introduce your new fur-child to his or her **assigned spot or place.** **Placement** is also a safe "timeout space" for your pet. You could encourage your pet to go there by putting treats and toys. You can say, "go

to your spot" or "go to your place" to get them use to what this means. You can also work on with your dog to get them to their safe spot, like; their crate and you can say, "go to your house" or "go to you room". You can designate  a room or area and say, "Go to your room". Especially when you have visitors! "Please dog name, go to your room", by using hand signals, treats, patience and repetition. It's just a matter of time before they catch on.

Training with Treats

Have your dog work for treats. A good time to work with your dog for basic training is before they eat breakfast or dinner while they are a little bit hun-

gry. You could even have them work for their food during a good training session. All they need is a small sized treats. Other good times to work for their treats are in the middle of the day. It's not as effective if your dog has a full stomach.

The **smell is very intense for dogs.** They always know where the treats are on you, and they will be eager for their next command for another treat reward. Some dogs may be motivated by playing tug of war or catch and retrieve; as a reward to learn a new trick. In other words, each dog has their currency that they will want to work for as their reward.

Portion Control Regimen

Please calculate the calories in your treats as part of your pet's total daily calories to your dogs breed size and consider natural fresh vegan food treats.

Look at this dog's face in reaction to the treat's smell. With a good treatment you can lure a dog to do just about anything!

Training Sessions

Understanding what motivates your dog for a reward is the key to a successful training session. It could be his or her favorite toy, rope, something bouncing like; a ball or kong toy. This can be equal to a treat reward.

- After a while of working with your dog, you can slowly stop using food or toys, but always use praise. A nice long stroke along the side, under neck and with a positive tone say, "good boy or girl".

- Dogs have short attention spans, so **keep each training session short.**

- **Use verbal praise**, physical reassurance, and an instant reward to reinforce initial training.

- **Treat Lure - Use sight of smell with food** to help get your dog to do just about anything with a good treat lure.

- Dogs learn by **repetition and reward.** As soon as they do what you want them too, then reward them.

- Always use a leash to ensure control.

- Cancel your training session if you or your

dog are tired.

- Always end each training session on a **positive encouraging note** and giving them a play session.

- You will need to use food rewards at first to enforce your commands. A hungry dog is an alert dog and will be ready to respond. **Make the treat visible,** but do not offer your dog any, until he or she carries out the command.

- First, get your dog to sit when they see it. Have your dog sit on verbal command, then slowly offer no food, only praise. You should work until the word commands are achieved. Then your hand signals will enforce the commands. This will happen gradually through daily regular practice.

- Remember that dogs learn by repetition, treats, praises, lots of patience, understanding and your dedication. You get what you put into your training sessions with your pet.

- When you work with a trainer, you will be the one getting trained and your dog is getting rehabilitation. The owner of the dog needs to be involved in working with their dog; for the dog to respond well to their commands.

Collar Choices

Collars are made from leather, rope, or mesh nylon. Check the length of the collar around the dog's neck. Make sure it does not catch on a long haired dog and that the dog can not get out of it, or snap off.

Check Chain and Martingale *on the right-side images.* You should be able to slip two fingers under a well-fitted collar. The collar will not slip off, in case the dog tugs backward on their leash.

Note: Each day, put your puppy's first collar on for only short periods of time, so they will grow up getting used to it. Remove the collar when you cannot supervise the puppy. As the puppy grows in size, check the collar size and change as needed.

While your dog is on the leash, *move the collar "high up" on the neck towards the head.* This allows you to control your dog and direct him/her in the direction that you want them to go.

Check Chain

When out walking, especially if they are around children or other dogs with short attention spans, a check chain or check collar is ideal for quick control.

Hold the check chain open in a circle and gently slip it over the dog's head. It should hang loosely around their neck. Dogs respond to a check chain collar, when the chain makes noise, as you pull up on the leash and it tightens. This is excellent for training your dog to walk with you and not ahead of you.

Head Holster

A head holster is ideal for strong bold dogs or for dogs that chew too much. Made of strong nylon, it clips onto a leash via a holster around the dog's nose and jaw. If the dog pulls or lunges, the momentum pulls their head down. This is an alternative to a check chain.

Harness

A harness for a small dog slips over the body and around the chest. The leash is attached over the dog's back to avoid collar pressure on the neck. Harnesses are used for dogs in pulling mega amounts of weight in dog pulling competitions. This also puts the dogs in a body position to lunge and to attack other dogs.

If you have a dog that pulls, this might make your dog pull more and you will have a tight leash, giving you a difficult time of being pulled and worn out. This behavior could make other dogs and people scared of your dog.

Police Leash

You can use this leash 3 different ways, doubles up as a regular leash, wrapped around your waist or the way police use it, hand free, over the shoulder. You can even use it for training the coma command, coming up in this book!

Choke Collar Training

Staring with my dog actor: "Papa Pretzel"! Choke Collar Information Training Video

Basic Commands

These basic commands are the foundation for all trick training.

Name
Use your dog's name whenever you are happy or offering something positive: like a treat or toy. Do not use it, if your dog will be disappointed with what comes next like; isolation or medication.

Name, Let's Go
Pat your hip for this command. It encourages your dog to follow or come to you.

Name Heal
This is the brother command to, *"let's go"*, instructing your dog to walk directly to your left heel.

No Sir or Ma'am

Good for everything you consider naughty, such as: grabbing on to unacceptable belongings, jumping and pulling, sidewalk crotch sniffing and all other not so endearing little habits.

Sit and Stay

Getting your dog to first; *"hold, sit and pay attention"* is an important beginning part of your tricks and reward treating training.

Wait, Stay and Okay

This is the sister command to "*sit and stay*". This will instruct your dog to stand still and stop momentarily at doors, curbs, thresholds and serves as a quick reminder that you are the leader.

Down

This command instructs your dog to lay down, a necessary position for tricks like; *"roll over, crawl, play dead"* and others tricks.

No Jumping

If your dog is excited and jumps on you, your family or friends, you must have control over your dog, before you start working with them.

Here is what to do when a friend, or family member, comes over to visit and becomes face to face with your dog, and they want to jump up on them:

- **HANDS and ARMS CROSSED in front of you.** (No Swinging of the Arms)

- **Turn away or walk backing up** - Everyone else in the household should do the same: in avoiding their attention in teaching your dog to not jump up on you or them again.

Tips: For some dogs, simply by holding something in their mouth during a greeting may just do the trick! So try giving your dog a preferred stuffed toys, balls, or have a long-lasting chew handy, when you have visitors over the next time.

- **If your dog jumps at you when you come home,** walk or back out and wait 30 seconds to 1 minute, then walk back in to calmly re-greet your dog. The moment your dog **jumps on you**, walk away again and close the door. Keep doing this, until your dog no longer jumps up on you. At this point, you can reward your dog; by **not** leaving and pet them.

- **Praise** When your dog has all four paws on the floor, give him attention and praise. If he jumps up at any point, freeze (with your arms folded across your chest), until they calm down.

Eye Contact

Have your dog, make eye contact with you before you go anywhere. The repetition of eye contact is so important. Treats and positive reinforcements are great rewards for good behavior. This is the most important fundamental part of your training.

Sit, Eye Contact and Stay

Using a treat will assist with these commands because of your dog's sense of smell is very strong. This can get them motivated to work for you. **Place the treat right over them,** making sure your dog does not jump up on you to get it. Pull the treat

away, if he/she does, until you get your **"sit"** command. **Then, reward and praise your dog.**

Look at the picture above, where my younger black big puppy dog looks towards my tan "helper dog" to show him the ropes of how to a "sit and lay down" on command exercise.

The *"Sit"* Command

Always have your pet sit and stay, before you give them any food treats. Have them remain in *"stay"* command until you tell them, it's *"ok"*, and then reward them. The *"sit"* command is the first and easiest command for your dog to learn.

- Practice first with a leash.

- Start the session with a food reward.

- Aim to make your dog sit by word alone.

Dogs respond to food held in front of the middle of your body.

1) Hold the food directly **above your dog's head**.

2) As your dog reaches, move your right hand up and over their head. In other words, **move the treat from the dog's nose to behind their head.** This will make his or her hind legs bend while they keep their eyes on the food treat. Give the command *"sit"*.

3) As your dog's bottom touches the floor, **place your hand on your dog's lower backside** and have them stay in place for about 30 seconds. This way they will associates this position of sitting with your command.

- Always give the command "sit" when you see your dog is about to sit. Practice this again and from the side. Reduce the number of treat rewards each time.

- If your dog refuses to sit, even with a treat, try walking them around on the leash a little bit to **reset** the *"sit"* session. Then restart and try to ease them into the *"sit"* command again. You can also **kneel and hold their collar with your right hand up**, as your dog should be on your left side. Remember to reward your dog with praise and a treat. Repeat the steps and progress to just giving praise alone, until they respond to this.

The *"Down"* Command

This a very important command for your dog to learn. It teaches your dog that you are in control. It is a good command to use when there are a lot of distractions.

There are two lay down positions:
The "**Sphinx**" (where the hind legs are tucked under the body) and the "**flat**" (where the hips and the legs are on one side). Both positions are natural for your dog.

The end of the leash should be held securely under your knees; if you are in a sitting position.

If your dog will not lay down, please be patient and kneel beside your pet on your left side.

1) Give your dog the *"sit"* command; besides you on your left side. Hold your dog's collar to slightly restrain them. As a lure, keep the treat visible in your other (right) hand.

2) ***Place the treat on your dog's nose and then move it downward. As your dog sniffs the treat, move the treat forward to the front of their body***. This will cause your dog to move downward.

3)As you move the treat forward (in a L shape motion) your dog should naturally start to stretch forward and lay down. Praise and reward your dog!

Repeat this exercise: until you get a good lay down response to your verbal *"lay down"* command, then later without a treat. You will have to encourage them to first get into a begging position. You may want to keep saying your pet's name for reassuring and praising them.

4) Ease your dog to the ground by gently pressing on their body and pulling their legs gently forward while keeping the pressure on their shoulders for a few seconds to relax them. Once you do this, they will lay down.

Comforting Contact - Praise your dog by giving them long strokes along their body; using the palms of your hand to make long even strokes. This makes an emotional connection.

Lay Down Under the Bridge

First, get your dog in the *"sit" command*, then show the treat under your leg to bring their body down. Then move the treat forward to complete the full lay down. Moving the leash downward and in a forward direction aids in achieving this.

"Lay Down" Hand Commands
Can Lead to Verbal
"Play Dead!" or "BANG!"

Leash Pulling

Pulling on the leash is the most common problem faced by dog owners. The remedy is to restrain with the **"*heal/come*"** command. Do not try to match your strength against the dog, as this may only get your dog to pull even more. Just get your dog to first; *stop, sit and stay,* before walking forward again.

A simple way to help your dog learn to walk without pulling on the leash is to **stop moving forward** when they start to pull. Always reward your dog with a treat when they walk by your side and sit/stay correctly. If your dog is not very interested in food treats, then you can use a tug toy or a ball for them in place of a treat.

1) Walk your dog on your left side and hold the leash with both hands. The right-hand holds the end and your left-hand guilds your dog. As your dog pulls, slide your left hand down the leash and then pull firmly upwards. Pull back firmly once. (Do not move forward and then come to a complete stop). Tell your dog to, "*stop*".

2) With your dog now in the correct heel position, command them to "*sit*". Begin to walk again, only after you got them to completely "sit". Then start to

walk again. This is a great time to use the *"heel"* command to get them to follow your lead when, walking them on a leash.

3) Repeat the *"heel"* and *"sit"* position, each time your dog pulls forward ahead of you. Make sure you make eye contact with your furry friend, so they know you have treats and it keeps their attention on you. Treats are always a great motivator and it gives them direction.

When your dog starts to walk to the *"heel"* command, without food rewards; try again. Anticipate ahead or when, your dog might pull. Then get his attention by making only a sound, so they will know to *"heel"*.

The *"Heel"* Command

Teaching your dog to walk on the *"heel"* command is a key part of obedience training, are an asset and a prime duty for dog owners. Some owners like to start with keeping rewards such as; your dog's favorite ball, teddybear or snacks handy to enforce commands.

1) Start training indoors. Kneel in front of your dog and let your dog smell the treat. Attach the leash to their collar and be sure not to apply any tension to the leash; as of yet.

2) Now give the *"sit"* command. With the leash in your left hand, hold the leash and a food reward in your right hand with no tension on the leash. Maintain slack in your left hand. You do not want to have a tight leash, otherwise, you will not have your dog's attention or control.

3) Walk with your dog beside you. Then give the command, *"heel"*. If your dog surges forward, gently pull back on their leash.

4) When your dog heels, give them a tidbit of a treat. Keep eye contact and say, your dog's name and then, *"good dog"*. Give the command to "sit" and repeat with praise, ***"good dog"***. Start to increase the distance as your dog obeys the sequence of the

"heel" command. You can increase distance with a 20-foot rope as part of a special *"come"* command exercise drill; (explained more in detail soon).

5) Try a simple turn to the right. Guide the dog around to your right with your left hand and give them the command, **"heel"**. By using your **left** hand to hold the leash, it leaves the handler's **right** hand free to signal. Traditionally, many dog activities rely on training a dog from the left. You should pick a side and stick with it. Your dog will then, know where they are suppose to walk and to not cross in front of you; surely to avoid you from tripping over them as well.

6) To make a left turn, increase your speed and hold a treat in front of your dog's nose to slow them down. Keep your dog close to your left leg and give the com-

mand, "*steady*", to help slow them down. Keep your dog close to your left leg at all times. Holding the back of your dog's collar or short leash and collar up will also help to maneuver your dog.

9/4/13 Urgent status; this 3 years old, Mastiff female only had 48 hours to find a foster or adopter when I took this picture at the shelter.

Feeding Your Pets

Dogs can develop problems of resource guarding food and sometimes this can lead a serious issue.

Check out this video of some of my 6 months old puppies fosters learning to; *"sit"*, *"stay"* and to "wait" for eating permission signaling with the clapping of my hand's command for their dinner.

Puppy Feeding Training Video!

"Give Me Five", "Paw" or "Paws Up"

Try this *"paws up"* exercise every day, at the same

time. Using repetition helps train a dog. Use a reward to motivate them when they give you their paw. You show your dog this command simply by grabbing their paw in your hand and say, "give me paw" and immediately after rewarded them. A **trainer's clicker** can be used to inform your dog that they did well and is getting a treat! When you call your dog's name and they come, give them a treat. When your dog heels, give them a tidbit of a treat. Keep your eye contact when saying your dog's name or "good dog". Then give the command, "sit", repeat and reward. It's fun!

Scheina

Check out this super smart girl at the Palm Beach County Animal Care and Control shelter shaking paws with me. ID #A1559513 on 1/12/14.

The *"Come"* Command

Dogs respond to food held in front and held in the middle of your body.

1- Place your dog in the sitting position and give the command, *"sit-wait"*. Avoid the word *"stay"* because your dog might get it confused with the *"stay"* with a *"wait"* until you

return command; or just remain standing with your palms open towards them.

2- In the *"sit"* command, draw the full length of the leash away from your dog and face the dog. Show them the food reward and call their name; adding the command *"come"*.

Remember to always hold the treat directly over the dog's head.

3- As soon as the dog reaches you; praise them and then give the command, *"sit"*. Repeat this step a few times for practice.

4- Practice the *"come"* command over greater distances with your dog and with a longer leash (even a long rope). Each time and further away from you. Use a toy reward that your dog can see from a distance rather than offering food.

A long line with slack can be pulled to ensure compliance.

5- When your dog obediently responds to the *"come"* and *"sit"* commands, give your dog praise and make a big fuss over it! Try not to overdo too many food rewards. **Make sure your dog sits obediently before they receive a reward.**

6- To make a left turn, increase your speed and hold a treat in front of your dog's nose to slow them down. Keep your dog close to your left leg and give the command, *"steady"* or *"easy"*, to help slow them down.

Keep your dog close to your legs (at all times) and hold the back of your dog's collar.

The "Roll Over" Trick

Once you have achieved the *"lay down"* command with your dog, you can now add the *"rollover"* command trick to it.

First, have your dog in a complete *"lay down"* position. Then by using a treat or toy of your dog's interest, position it over their head (so they can still see it), then move it to your dog's opposite side for them to complete the full *"roll-over"* command.

The *"Stay"* and *"Up"* Command

Once you get your dog in the *"lay down" command*, your dog will be ready for their *"get up"* command. Use the smell of the treat to lure your dog up. Follow with the verbal command and then praise them! Repeat.

Mix It Up a Bit and Have Fun

When your pets understand the *"sit"* and *"stay"* commands, you can then have one of your dogs *"sit", "stay" at* a stationary regular training spot. Then use your other dog for the drills: like walking around the other dog that is sitting and staying still, or you can have one dog jump, as the other sits/stays for some fun. They should each take turns in the training, and this is an excellent way to practice the *"stay"* command and get to do some play drills with your fur-children. It's a win-win situation for everyone!

Canine Good Citizen

The AKC's Canine Good Citizen program is the gold standard of behavior for dogs in our communities. This is a non-competitive test to recognize and certify dogs and their owners as responsible citizens.

Developed and promoted by the American Kennel Club, their goal is to encourage pet owners to learn the skills necessary to train their dogs to be safe and well-mannered members of our society.

To pass this test, your dog must know the basic commands of; *"heal"*, *"sit"*, *"down"* and *"stay"*. The test is composed of the following 10 evaluations:

1. **Accepting a friendly stranger:** To pass this test your dog must allow a non-threatening person to approach and speak to their handler.

2. **Sitting politely for petting:** Your dog must allow a friendly stranger to touch him/her while sitting at their handler's side.

3. **Allowing basic grooming procedures:** Your dog must be clean, well-groomed, and must allow a stranger (representing a veterinarian or groomer) to handle and groom him/her without any problems.

4. **Walking on a loose leash:** Going out for walks; your dog must walk tentatively at their handler's, side to pass this evaluation.

5. **Walking through a crowd:** Your dog must be attentive to their owner and be in control as they are led through a crowd of people.

6. **Sit and down on command/stay in place:** Your dog must respond to their handler's, *"sit"*, *"down"* and *"stay"* commands.

7. **Coming when called:** A test to ensure your dog is reliable to come to you when you call him or her.
8. **React appropriately to other dogs:** Your dog must be in control and focused on their handler when passing other dogs.

9. **React appropriately to distractions:** Your dog must remain calm and confident when faced with everyday distractions. The distractions at an evaluation may include a child running, a bicyclist, a person on crutches or in a wheelchair.

10. **Supervise supervision:** Calmly enduring a supervised a separation from the owner. For this test; a stranger will hold your dog by their leash and is expected to wait calmly when their handler disappears for three minutes.

If all ten objectives are met, the handler can apply for a certificate and a special dog tag from the AKC; stating that the dog has earned the CGC!

Dogs do not have to be registered with the AKC to earn a CGC, nor do they have to be purebred, nor be registered with any canine organization. The goal is to promote good citizenship for all dogs.

Schutzhund

Here is a video of a friend of mine training a couple of dogs for championship competition.

Schutzhund Training Video!

Schtzhund (German for "protection dog") is a dog sport that was developed in Germany in the early 1900s as a breed suitability test for the German

Shepherd breed today with Belgian Malinois. The test would determine if the dog displayed the appropriate traits and characteristics of a proper working German Shepherd. Today it is used as a sport where many breeds, other than German Shepherd dogs, can compete. It is such a demanding test, that only a few dogs can pass. Nowadays, they are training from Schutzhund to Pitbulls as well!

Schutzhund tests dogs of all breeds for the traits necessary for police-type work. Dogs that pass Schutzhund tests should be suitable for a wide variety of tasks: police work, specific odor detection, search and, and many others. The purpose of Schutzhund is to identify dogs that, have or do not have the character traits required for these demanding jobs. Some of those traits are:

Strong desire to work, courage, intelligence, trainability, strong bond to their handler, perseverance, protective instinct, sense of smell, strength, endurance, agility and their scent ability.

Chapter 9
Dog Attack Facts

Dogbite.org studies: 1982 & 2014

- 4.5 - 4.7million people have been bitten by dogs in the United States. That is 2% of the US population. One out of every five bites become infected.

- 50% of kids will be bitten by age 12. Almost one in five people bitten by dogs will require medical attention.

- Every year, more than 800,000 Americans receive medical attention for dog bites; at least half of them are children.

- Annual data from 2014, shows that 48% (20) of the fatality victims were children 13 years and younger; 52% (22) were adults (20-years and older). Of the total adults killed by dogs in 2014, 73% (16) were ages 50 years and older.

- In 2014, 19% (8), of all dog bite fatality victims were either visiting or living temporarily with the dog's owner when the fatal attack occurred (down from 38% in 2013). Children 6 years and younger accounted for 88% (7) of these deaths.

- 57% (24) of all fatalities in 2014, involved more than one dog; 19% (8) involved a pack attack of four or more dogs; 31% (13) involved breeding on the dog owner's property (either actively or in the recent past) and 5% (2) involved tethered dogs.

- 76% of the attacks resulted in fatalities.

- Dog ownership information for 2014, shows that family dogs comprised 48% (20) of all fatal attack occurrences; 40% (17) of the attacks occurred off the dog owner's property, up from 22% in 2013; 21% (9) resulted in criminal charges.

- 77% of dog bites are from the pet of the family or friends; 50% of attacks occurred on the dog owner's property.

- 86% results in maiming - it's very common for dog owners to get bit while breaking up their dogs from fighting.

- Most dog bites affecting young children, occurred during everyday activities or while, interacting with familiar dogs. **Never leave your child alone**. Even though your dog is a good dog, they can be easily provoked. Senior citizens are the second most common dog, bite victims.

- 6% of attacks result in fatalities.

- In the 1980's and 1990's, the United States averaged 17 fatalities per year. In the 2000's, this has increased to 26 fatalities: 77% of dog bites are from the pet of their family or friends.

- 50% of the occur on the dog owner's property.

- Animal bites, most of which are from dogs, are 1% of the reasons for visits to the emergency room in the United States.

5 Dog Breeds That Bite but Are Almost Never Reported

- Dachshund
- Chihuahua
- Jack Russel Terrier
- Cocker Spaniel
- Yorkshire Terrier

Walking Safely

Prevention, Defense and Protection
- Do not walk a dog that, is too big for you to restrain. You do not have control of a dog if, the dog can pull you off your feet, or drags you where your

pet wants to go. The same caution applies for letting your child hold the leash, or walk a dog alone.

- Do not use a ***retractable leash***, unless it's safe for your dog to lunge the full length of the leash (away from you), and always have one hand occupied in holding the box part. Many dogs have been run over because, retractable leashes allowed dogs to dash into the street. Many dogs run off in a panic when the owner dropped the box, then fleeing even further to escape this plastic object that, is following them (the retractable leash box). Also, if the retractable leash gets tangled while meeting another dog, this could result in a fight that, otherwise would not have taken place.

- It's better not to do "dog to dog" greetings when walking your dog unless you know both the dogs are good at greeting other dogs on a leash because, they know they can not flee, if they need too. Leashed dogs can be defensive when meeting new dogs on a leash. The same goes for letting children greet or pet your leashed dog.

- When walking your dog, it is most important to be familiar with the territory that, you are planning to walk. Some people may have loose dogs on their property; their dogs may be very protective guard

dogs, and it may be too late before you could avoid a possible dog attack. If you are walking past bushes, you could be walking right into a loose dog: ready to attack! They may have heard you coming from down the street and are already in a position to attack you and your dog.

- Chances are that an attacking dog will first becoming at your dog and then you. If you have more than one dog, this could heighten the attack and be more dangerous; Your dogs could all get loose and cause an accident. It is important to know what is around you so that, you can avoid a confrontation with any loose dogs.

- Always assume, if you can't see what is ahead of you, that there could be a situation, just a few feet from you that, you may be walking into. Corners can be very dangerous; if you can't see what is around the corner, you don't know what you could be running into. Always keep your space and distance so that, you are not putting you and your dog at risk. Remember this can leave you with very little time to respond and in a dangerous situation.

- **Avoid walking past fenced yards with dogs** because, the dogs on the property could jump, climb the fence, or even dig a hole real fast to get at you. If you see a dog trying to jump a fence, it is from the other side of the street and firmly and calmly tell the dog, "No!" Every dog should know the **"No"** word. Repeat and repeat again!

- **Avoid walking on county roads,** train tracks, vacant lots, field or anywhere dogs may roam free.

- **Never trust other people walking their dog,** especially if the leash looks tight from the dog pulling, or lunging away them. This will only make the dog want to lunge toward you more. Dog owners think that their dog would never bite, but that is not always true.

- **Give special attention when you are coming around a corner:** Again, always be prepared for anything. You might find yourself heading right into a loose dog that heard you coming and you may have little time to react defensively. Do not walk your dog too far ahead of you. Keep them on a 4-6 ft. leash at most because you would be putting your dog in a situation you can't avoid. By coming too close and too fast into an unknown attacking dog is very startling. This is a good reason to not wear head seats with loud music playing.

- **When night walking, you need to always be visible**. Have your dog wear a reflective dog collar, leash tags and clothing, so that cars and people can see you and your dog. Have a **flashlight** handy, so that you can see where you are walking. LED blinking flash lights work best.

- I recommend carrying an **"electric whistle"** or a "taser". Test it before every walk and make sure you have a fully charged battery, and it works. When a dog hears the taser's noise (based on my experience), the attacking dog will usually back off and head in the other direction. Always have your taser easily accessible. If using a pepper or citronella spray, you will need to aim for their nose. Practice with it first, so you know it works, how far the range, and how to use it properly. Pepper sprays can have harmful results to you and your pet if the wind is blowing the wrongs direction. Keep in mind you can make the dog more agitated.

- A horn or a pet compressor can also make a situation worse: if not used with proper timing, but this can be very effective.

- My personal opinion is that pepper spray is an inhumane correction method to use when you are being attacked. I prefer to carry my taser because, the unfamiliar sound, scares them away when they hear it. It would hurt the dog, but dogs Just yell at them, *"no"* and *"stop"*, before they are too close to your dog or you.

What to do When You See a Loose Dog

There are many different levels of dog confrontations. When you first see a loose dog, do not make direct eye contact and keep them in your peripheral vision because a dog could feel threatened and then attack. Do not scream, as it could scare the dog even more.

- Avoid sudden movements. Do not smile, flail your hands, or jump around; especially children.

- Do not walk towards the dog's direction.

- As soon as you see a loose dog, stop and do not run. If you do the dog may run after you or your child because of their instinct to do so. The dog is always going to be faster than you.

- Never turn your back from the dog. It can turn into a charging dog, so always keep your eye on the dog.

- Remain motionless, hands at your sides and avoid direct eye contact with the dog so that, you can identify what kind of situation you are in.

Most Common Signs Dogs Give Before Biting in Any Situation

It is important to learn to assess the situation within a few seconds and identify what the dog's body language and behavior are saying; before any potentially dangerous situation gets out of hand.

As soon as the dog hears or sees you coming around the corner, they will be sizing you up. This will take about 3 seconds for you to identify your situation to react and to get them to snap out of it, or break out their *"tunnel vision"* before they go to bite you. This happens very quickly, so you must always be on alert for you and your dog's safety.

Read the following warning signs:

- The dog moves a step back, ears are flat back, then they turn their head, like saying that they need space, they may lick their lips (which means that they are in distress), or sniff before they go to bite you.

- Tensed body, a stiff tail, pulled back head and/or ears, furrowed brow, eyes rolled so the whites are visible, yawning, flicking tongue, intense stare or backing away in any situation.

- Signs of aggression. Such as; growling, snarling, baring teeth and lunging are easy to read. There can also be signs that, are very subtle. Such as; a moment of tension, a wagging tail (does not always mean their happy to see you. He could be happy to bite you!). Walking back, cowering down, tucked tail, barking and moving toward you.

Growling, crouching, lip biting, tucked tail, snapping, licking lips and lunging toward another dog or backing away are all signs to use extra caution.

If you, even using extra caution, notice a dog has tunnel vision on you or object: he is probably going to attack.

What to do if a Dog is Heading Towards You Aggressively

- Avoid eye contact

- You must break tunnel vision

- Turn your body slowly to the side.

- Cross your arms

- Completely ignore the dog

- Be still for a short period, then move slowly away.

- Try to get to a place where there is a barrier between you and the dog.

- Place a board or anything you can find between you and the dog.

- Spray the dog with a water bottle, or water hose.

- Bang to make noise on an object, or blow an air horn.

- Use the commands, *"no"* and *"stop"*.

- Toss a blanket, towel, your shirt, or anything you can find over the top of them.

- Yelling at them will only make the dog react more.

Protection
What To Do Before a Dog Starts to Attack You!

If the dog continues to come towards you and makes direct eye contact, do not stand head-on with the dog. This can frighten the dog, so just **turn your body at an angle.** With a firm and dominate loud voice say, **"stop",** with your hand in front of you, gesturing with your fingers spread wide apart. **Continue to say, "no" and "stop"**, (every dog should know "no"). If needed, clap your hands and pound your foot firmly on the ground. Repeat as needed. Hopefully, the dog's owner will hear this, and will come out, or someone else will come to help you when they hear the dog barking.

- **Command your space**

- **Stay calm** and do not scream. Screaming could easily antagonize the dog more.

- **Once the dog loses interest in you, slowly back away,** until he is out of sight. Keep your eyes on him, until you get yourself out of the situation. Contact your local animal services immediately.

- ***Feed the dog your jacket, purse, bicycle or anything that you can put between yourself and the dog for protection. Shield yourself and*** *call for help.* In other words, give them something else to bite and find something to shield yourself.

- **Throw a shirt, towel, blanket, or something to** *cover his vision*. Hopefully, this will keep the dog busy so that you can getaway.

If you fall, or are knocked to the ground, which is common, *curl up into a ball* or roll around. Put your hands over your head, cover your face, neck and abdomen area. Remain motionless and try not to scream. At this point, it could make it worse.

How to Defend Yourself From an Attacking Dog

Dog attacks are a very dangerous situation. Be prepared to defend yourself with some of the safety devices that, I mentioned earlier, even if it means unavoidable lethal force. Take cautious measures to protect yourself because, it could be the attacking dog, or you.

- Hitting the dog will only excite the dog even more. Try to act as calmly as possible. If you are witnessing a fight, you can end it by covering the dog's head with a blanket, jacket or shirt. Blocking the dog's vision will normally cause a dog to disengage.

- If you are not prepared, then look for anything to use to defend yourself such as garbage can lids (as a shield), a rake, bag or a shirt. Use anything handy as a barrier between you and the attacking dog. You can get them to bite your purse or backpack instead of you. An umbrella can be used as a weapon or shield. Sometimes opening and closing an umbrella in the dog's face might deter him. Find a nearby car or fence to get behind or climb onto.

- If you have to hit the dog, hit him between the shoulder blades or head.

- Only if you have a clear kick, use everything you have to protect yourself. Be careful that, the dog does not turn around and bite your leg.

- Kick a small dog in the nose. The nose is a very sensitive area and this may deter the dog from biting.

- ***If a dog is going to bite you give him your weaker arm*** so that you can use your dominant hand to strike and fight them off. From there, with you needed to protecting yourself while the dog has a hold on your weaker arm), you have to know where to hit the dog for a quick release. Go for a sharp strike with everything you have; between the shoulders blade in the spine area, or go under the throat of the dog to cause a vomit reaction.

As difficult as this may be, try not to pull away from the dog biting you because **this will only make the dog more aggressive and tear into your skin. Instead, grab the back of their head and press it against your arm.** This way they can not close their mouths (to deepen the injury). Pulling and screaming makes it worse.

How to Stop a Dog From Continuing to Attack a Victim

- **If you can, try aiming a water hose at the nose.**

- If a dog is attacking the victim, come around to the back of the dog and grab the collar firmly with both hands (if dog does not have collar; grab a belt or leash to use as a collar).

- Straddle the dog and immediately squeeze your knees into the dog to immobilize him.

- Twist the collar and then lift it. Squeeze firmly! Wait for the dog to choke a bit, to release their bite.

- Only then should you pull off. If you pull away while the dog is biting, it will cause more damage to the victim.

- If the dog will not let go, then push the bottom of the dog's neck firmly up to **choke them** and cause the dog to have a vomit reaction and will cause the dog to release the victim.

- **Always remain calm**. It is very dangerous to break up dog fights.

- It is more *common for the owners to get bitten by their own dogs.*

How to Stop a Dog Fight with 2 People

Pull them apart by the back legs, lift up and move in a circular direction so they don't bite you. Remember that a dog can turn and snap at you. Get a hold of the dog keep moving in circle and backward until you keep them from biting again. Spin fast enough, so the dog doesn't bite again. Lift them up in a wheelbarrow like position. If the dog comes at you at this moment, you may have to slam the dog onto the ground. Get the dogs stretched out, until one of them lets go, or someone else could even put a finger up their butt to; get them to let go of the other dog. Yes, that's right, this will snap them out of the attack mode and they will finally let go of the other dog! This is the most effective. Unless the dog is trained for fighting, this can work.

Some people are against this "pull back legs" technique, but it works very well for others. I always grab their legs; from up high, close to stomach up towards from their back side and stomach area of the dog's body so I don't hurt dog's legs. For an older dog, This may be safer to prevent hip injury to the dog.

Stopping a Dog Fight With 1 Person

Always know where at least 2 leashes are. If you are alone, have 2 dogs, or more fighting; wrap one leash under the belly and thread the latch part through the hand loop. Then wrap around their belly towards the hind legs and pull them up off the ground. If the dogs are still fighting, pull dogs to where you can secure the first dog: hook and latch him. Then try to do the same thing with the other dog. It may take some time for them to settle down, but it will happen.

- Better yet, if you have a special "police leash", you can use this, specially designed for these types of situations. You can easily hook it around their abdomen and back legs. Pull to tighten it and hook the leash to tree or door.

- Stay towards the back area of the dog and do not put your hands around their teeth.

- Use a "dressage whip" (specially designed not to hurt dogs and used as a training device) for dogs that, won't let go, to snap dog out of their attack mode.

- Break stick: A plastic 10-inch stake that, you can get at any hardware store. It can be used as break a break stick to pop the dog's mouth open. It is risky, but at last resort, you have to use something.

- Look for a proper fit when grabbing the collar to turn the dog's head and inserting it from the side, to keep the dog from being able to bite again. Keep the dog between your legs, with a tight hold on the collar to keep control of the dog's neck. Breaks stick can be used to get a dog to let go by first sliding it in the side of the dog's mouth to pry the jaws open. Some police have used a baton or screwdriver.

- Finger in up butt hole

What To Do Someone Gets Bitten by a Dog

Immediately wash the wound thoroughly with soap and warm water.

- Apply pressure and ice immediately to prevent swelling and bruising.

- Contact your physician for additional care and advice. Dogs can bite so hard that, it can cause bones to break and they may need an x-ray.

- Report the bite to your local animal care and control agency. Tell the animal control officer everything you can to avoid issues with other pet's owner directly. Animal services will collect all the rabies information on dog for you.

How to Avoid a Dog From Being a Dangerous Liability

Dog aggression issues start innocently enough and can be hard to detect if you don't know what signs to look for. It can happen very quickly and you must know what to do; to snap your dog out of the **"tunnel vision"** attack mode. Watch for dominant posture, that can be a "pre-attack" state of mind in a split second, so you can **be able to make the right corrections.** It can make the difference between a good or bad choice for your dog in the future.

Millions of dog owners deal with their dogs having issues within their own homes. This should be worked out with a professional trainer, that specializes in this, to avoid future reoccurrences of any dog attack situations. Also note that older dogs deal with internal, arthritic pain, social behavior and by bringing in a high energy puppy, it can irritate them and cause them to bite.

You should know that any breed of dog can bite. To prevent liabilities, you should master walking them on a leash as soon as possible. Practicing basic training skills will enable you to properly manage your dogs. What I mean is, by training your dogs the basic commands: *"sit"*, *"lay down"*, *"stay" and "come"*, you will be able to take your dog almost anywhere. Make sure first that, you have control of your dog. Your fur-child should be obedient to know that, you are the leader of the pack. Often dog owners are overcome by the power of their dog simply by not making early corrections or practicing basic commands while they are young because of lack of time. This can lead to many dangerous situations and issues. When it comes to the life of your pet, never leave anything to chance.

Spay and Neuter

Spay or neuter your dog, to lessen the risk of aggression problems at a later age. Sterilization is commonly done by the ages of 6-9 months. After 10-12 months, the dog may have already learned aggression. Having testosterone may have developed in their behavior issues. For a female, the first heat can be a traumatic experience because, of badgering by male dogs. The female can develop a learned defensive reaction to being approached by other dogs. Spaying her later will not change the learned behavior. This may also reduces the dog's chances of cancer.

Unfortunately, a study, performed by Dr. Benjamin L. Hart at the University of California, suggests that altered dogs have an increased chance of getting cancers such as; hemangiosarcoma, lymphoma, osteosarcoma, and mast cell tumors (MCT). The *Whole Dog Journal* adds that male dogs

who are neutered are also more prone to also developing prostate cancer.

About Your Dog

Introduce your dog at an early age to visitors to come in your home, community parks, family and friends; even the noise of playing children, busy sidewalks and other animals.

Make sure these experiences are positive and not frightening for them. The more your dog feels safe in a variety of situations, the less chance they will feel compelled to bite. An unsocialized dog can bite because they may feel threatened by new situations and even causing them to run away.

Exercise Your Dogs

All dogs need some daily physical exercise. This does not need to exhaust them, but it should make them pleasantly tired. Mental exercise is just as important, so your dog feels like they have had some interesting experiences threw out the course of their day. Bored dogs are more inclined to develop destructive behavior, than dogs whose life is active and interesting for at least an hour or two every day.

Train Your Dogs

It is important to use reward-based methods when training your dog and only voice reprimands when your dog does something naughty. Do not slap, hit, or kick your dog. Do not get angry over doggie's mistakes. Instead, try to help your dog understand what you want them to do. Provided you choose this kind of training, you can start when your fur-pup is only 7-8 weeks of age. This kind of training also works well with adult dogs. The **"come"** command, is the most important command that, your dog will ever learn. A dog who will unhesitatingly come to you when you call them can be taken out of any developing dangerous situation. For example; if you see your dog is becoming frightened or defensive, is heading for a busy street, chasing a child or a cat or is getting ready to go greet a dangerous dog: the situation can be neutralized just by the voiced *"come"* command.

Do not let your dog wander off in your neighborhood. Even if you have a non-aggressive type of dog. Their experiences while wandering could teach the dog to be aggressive. Wandering dogs often get killed by traffic, or can get shot by the police officers or your neighbors. If you want to have your dog out in the yard, be sure you have a fence that will contain your dog, and that will protect them from whatever passes by. It's very common for dogs to get stolen from people's property by strangers. Electric fences may teach dogs to be aggressive to passers-by (because the dog gets shocked if they go to greet them), and they do not protect your dog from dangers that could invade your yard. If a dog leaves an electric-fenced yard in a moment of excitement, they will hesitate to return because returning will mean getting another shock.

Chaining a dog not a good idea. Besides, it not being safe, because oftentimes dogs can get hurt severely. **Tethering is illegal in most cities.** This limits their ability to regulate social space and the knowledge that, they can't flee if they feel threatened. Feeling safe is important to dogs, just like human beings. If a dog can not get their distance from something is approaching them, they may feel no other choice, but to bite. In some cases, the chained dog may feel they have to desperately defend themselves. *A Denver study published in 1994, revealed that biters were nearly 3 times as likely to be chained as to being unchained.*

In the past 10-years, many jurisdictions have adopted anti-tethering ordinances as well. Chaining may not even be legal in your city or county.

Constrain Your Dogs

Do not let your dog wander off in your neighborhood. Even if you have a non-aggressive type of dog. Their experiences while wandering could teach the dog to be aggressive. Wandering dogs often get killed by traffic, or can get shot by the police or your neighbors. If you want to have your dog out in the yard, be sure you have a fence that will contain your dog and that will protect them from whatever passes by. It's very common for dogs  to get stolen from people's property by strangers. Electric fences may teach dogs to be aggressive to passers-by (because the dog gets shocked if they goes to greet them), and they do not protect your dog from dangers that could invade your yard. If a dog leaves an electric-fenced yard in a moment of excitement, they will hesitate to return because returning will mean getting another shock.

Chaining a dog is also not a good idea. Besides, it not being safe, tethering is illegal in most cities. This limits their ability to regulate social space and the knowledge that they can't flee, if they feel threatened. Feeling safe is important to dogs. If a dog can not get their distance from something is approaching them, they may feel no other choice, but to bite. In some cases, the chained dog may feel they have to desperately defend themselves and develop this behavioral patterns..*A Denver study published in 1994, revealed* that biters were nearly 3 times as likely to be chained as to be unchained. In the past 10-years, many jurisdictions have adopted anti-tethering ordinances as well. Chaining may not even be legal in your city or county.

Limit Exposure to Untested Situations or Places

If your dog is unfamiliar with busy sidewalks, joggers, playgrounds full of screaming children, a room full of unknown guests, then do not expose your dog to these situations, until you know these things will not frighten your dog. You can gradually train a dog not to fear such situations by socializing them as soon as possible. Simply throwing a dog in at the deep end can lead to a disaster.

If you consider your dog a 'family' dog, understand that the dog may still have to learn that, visitors are also welcomed in the house; not just everyday family members. Do everything you can to teach your dog that humans are trustworthy and not a danger. Make sure all of their experiences with humans are good ones. If in doubt, allow your dog to meet a new guest outdoors and become comfortable with that guest before going indoors together.

You may have your dog in their safe room to let them get use to your visitor's voice and watch you interact with them first.

Dog Parks

Many dogs enjoy socializing with their own kind at a dog park. However, dogs do not need to have other dog friends to lead a full and happy life. Do not take your dog to a dog park if you can not control them. People always bring dogs with aggression problems to the park and you, or your dog may not know. Instead, consider play dates with dogs that you do know and behave normally around other dogs. Do not take your dog to a dog park if you know that, your dog has aggression problems. Instead, make sure you do enough interesting things with him during each day, like, walks. Dogs need exercise for good for mind and body balance, rides and playing catch! Training with your dog is the best exercise. Your dog will be perfectly happy with this.

Reference research dogsbite.org

Good-Bye

Thank you for reading my book. I appreciated you spending time to learn more about dogs. They mean the world to me!

We need to help animals in shelters, rescues and everywhere that we can. Let's live in harmony on our journey into the future, along side all kinds of creatures on this earth.

I wish everyone, happy dog guardianship, knowledge, safety, health, love, happy memories and harmony on your journey into future living in alongside your furry friends and family members!

Open your heart to fostering, volunteering, donating for more veterinarian medical research, sterilizing, advocating and adopting a shelter dog!

Check out my other dog education books of my Everything Dogs Book Collection

By Mercy Lopez
www.everythingdogs.net

GETTING STARTED ON THE RIGHT PAW

B A S I C D O G T R A I N I N G

Introducing Your New Dog to Your Home, Other Pets and More!

This book goes over: How to Pick the Right Pet Together as a Family, Statistics, What to Consider When Adopting a Dog, True Shelter Dog's Pictures & Video Stories Links, Children and Dogs, How to Introduce Your New Dog to Your Home and Other Exciting Pets, How to Doggie Proof Your Home and Yard, How To Get Ready for Your New Dog to Come Home, Safety, House Training, Chewing, Leaving Pets Home Alone, How to Avoid Bathroom Accidents, Basic Dog Training, Placement, Rewards for Your Dogs, Basic Commands, Leash Pulling, Heel and more!

Everything Dogs Book Series Collection

- **Saving Shelter Dogs**
- **Getting Started on the Right Paw Basic Dog Training**
- **Dog Health Maintenance & Natural Holistic Remedies Encyclopedia**

By Mercy Lopez

www.everythingdogs.net